# *Minute Masterpieces*

*A collection of choice prose, poetry, and quotations to fit any mood.*

*Compiled by* . . LUCY GERTSCH

**BOOKCRAFT**

SALT LAKE CITY, UTAH

# MINUTE MASTERPIECES

35th Printing, 1993

Lithographed in U. S. A.
by
Publishers Press

# PREFACE

Under this cover, I have gathered some bits of philosophy, prose, and verse which have been inspirational to me. Among these writings are words of encouragement, words of comfort for the sorrowing, and words of wisdom for those who seek it. All emotions possible to the human heart today have been experienced before us. Hope, despair, love, hate, joy, sorrow, anger, regret, and pain are all part of living. My selections are from those women of warm understanding, whose words and deeds have helped others over the rough places.

The purpose of my compilation is two-fold—to have selections that have become meaningful to me, under one easily available cover, and to offer them to my friends in condensed form.

May this little volume find its way to you when you need it most. May it give you hope, inspiration, and determination to "carry on."

THE AUTHOR

# ACKNOWLEDGMENTS

The compiler gratefully acknowledges and gives deep appreciation for helpful criticisms and permission to use the following selected prose and poetry to:

Blodwen and Maxine Gertsch for help in typing the manuscript.

Carl Barrett for the poem, "Pride."

To Unity School of Christianity, Lee's Summit, Missouri, for "Twelve Rules of Happiness," "Twenty-Four Golden Hours," and "Cheese and Crackers."

Thomas Y. Crowell and Co., publishers for the Benjamin Franklin story, the quotation on opportunity, and for the story of Canova. These are all taken from "Pushing to the Front" by Orison Marden.

Curtis Publishing Co. and Mrs. B. Y. Williams for "Your House of Happiness." Reprinted by special permission from the *Ladies' Home Journal.*

Funk & Wagnalls for "No Enemies" from *Hoyt's New Encyclopedia of Practical Quotations.*

Grosset & Dunlap for quotations on "Self-Piety" by Mildred Seydell in "Chins Up."

Harper and Brothers for "Keeping His Word" from "75 Stories for the Worship Hour."

McGraw-Hill Publishing Co. for Naomi John White's "I Taught Them All."

Napoleon Hill for his six quotations.

Houghton and Mifflin Co. for Sill's poem, "Opportunity."

*Hoyt's New Encyclopedia of Practical Quotations* for "Enemies."

Nephi Jensen for his quotations.

The Judson Press for "The Brief Description of a Brief Life," taken from the book "The Real Jesus," by James Allan Francis.

W. Livingston Larned, *People's Home Journal,* and to the *Reader's Digest* for "Father Forgets."

*McCall's* and Bruce Barton for his poem, "Two Seas." (Copyright 1928 by *McCall's.*)

W. B. McConkie Publishing Co., Division of Rand-McNally & Co., for the following poems of Ella Wheeler Wilcox: "Which Are You?" "You Can Never Tell," "Worth while," and "Optimism."

Joy Elmer Morgan, editor of the *Journal of the National Education Association of the United States* for excerpt from P. G. L. No. 42, Franklin's plan on "Self-Improvement," and for "Vanquished Friend."

Reilly & Lee Co. for "Myself," from the book of collected verse by Edgar A. Guest, copyright 1934, "The Spoiled Boy," by Edgar A. Guest, copyright 1936, and "Sermons We See" by Edgar A. Guest.

Jessie B. Rittenhouse for his poem "My Wage" from "The Door of Dreams," Houghton Mifflin Co., publishers.

Virginia Stillman for permission to use her two poems, "Onward" and "Triumph."

Margaret L. White, former supervisor of Language Arts in Elementary Grades.

Mrs. Emily Whitney Smith for O. F. Whitney's essay.

# TABLE OF CONTENTS

# TABLE OF CONTENTS (Cont.)

*Page*

# President George Albert Smith's Creed

I would be a friend to the friendless and find joy in ministering to the needs of the poor.

I would visit the sick and afflicted and inspire in them a desire for faith to be healed.

I would teach the truth to the understanding and blessing of all mankind.

I would seek out the erring one and try to win him back to a righteous and a happy life.

I would not seek to force people to live up to my ideals but rather love them into doing the thing that is right.

I would live with the masses and help to solve their problems that their earth life may be happy.

I would avoid the publicity of high positions and discourage flattery of thoughtless friends.

I would not knowingly wound the feeling of any, not even one who may have wronged me, but would seek to do him good and make him my friend.

I would overcome the tendency to selfishness and jealousy and rejoice in the success of all the children of my Heavenly Father.

I would not be an enemy to any living soul.

Knowing that the Redeemer of mankind has offered to the world the only plan that will fully

develop us and make us happy here and here-
after, I feel it not only a duty but also a blessed
privilege to disseminate the truth.

# BLESSINGS

## BLESSINGS IN DISGUISE

Our greatest blessings often come in disguise.
The experiences that gratify selfish longings are
not the ones that do us the largest good . . .

*" 'Tis sorrow builds the shining ladder up,*
*Whose golden rounds are our calamities."*

Who has read but to admire Emerson's great
essay on "Compensation?" A few paragraphs
from that masterpiece of profound thought and
eloquent expression are here presented:

The changes that break up at short intervals
the prosperity of men are advertisements of a
nature whose law is growth. Evermore it is the
order of nature to grow, and every soul is by this
intrinsic necessity quitting its whole system of
things . . . as the shellfish crawls out of its beautiful but stony case, because it no longer admits
of its growth, and slowly forms a new house.
. . . Then there can be enlargement, and the man

of today scarcely recognizes the man of yesterday . . .

The compensations of calamity are made apparent to the understanding also, after long intervals of time. A fever, a mutilation, a cruel disappointment, a loss of wealth, a loss of friends seems at the moment unpaid loss, and unpayable. But the sure years reveal the deep remedial force that underlies all facts. The death of a dear friend, wife, brother, lover, which seemed nothing but privation, somewhat later assumes the aspect of a guide or genius; for it commonly operates revolutions in our way of life, terminates an epoch of infancy or of youth which was waiting to be closed, breaks up a wanted occupation, or a household, or a style of living, and allows the formation of new ones more friendly to the growth of character. It permits or constrains the formation of new acquaintances, and the reception of new influences that prove of the first importance of the next years; and the man or woman who would have remained a sunny garden flower, with no room for its roots and too much sunshine for its head, by the falling of the walls and the neglect of the gardener, is made the banian of the forest, yielding shade and fruit to wide neighborhoods of men . . .

Our strength grows out of our weakness. Not until we are pricked and stung and sorely shot at, awakens the indignation which arms itself with secret forces. . . . Blame is safer than praise.

Joseph Smith, long before Ralph Waldo Emerson, taught the great doctrine of "Compensation."' The Prophet was lying in a dungeon, in the mob-ridden state of Missouri. His people had been despoiled and driven, and he, with a few faithful friends, had been thrown into prison, where he spent the dreary winter of 1838-39. In the agony of his soul he called upon God for deliverance, and was answered in these precious words:

"My son, peace be unto thy soul; thine adversity and thine affliction shall be but a small moment.

"And then, if thou endure it well, God shall exalt thee on High; thou shalt triumph over all thy foes.

"If you are called to pass through tribulations; if thou art in perils among false brethren; if thou art in perils among robbers; if thou art in perils by land or by sea;

"If thou art accused with all manner of false accusations; if thine enemies fall upon thee; if they tear thee from the society of thy father and mother and brethren and sisters; and if with a drawn sword thine enemies tear thee from the bosom of thy wife, and of thine offspring

. . . and thou be dragged to prison, and thine enemies prowl around thee like wolves for the blood of the lamb;

"And if thou shouldst be cast into the pit, or into the hands of murderers, and the sentence of death passed upon thee; if thou be cast into the deep; if the billowing surge conspire against thee; if fierce winds become thine enemy; if the heavens gather blackness, and all the elements combine to hedge up the way; and above all, if the very jaws of hell shall gape open the mouth wide after thee, know thou, my son, that all these things shall give thee experience, and shall be for thy good.

"The Son of Man hath descended below them all. Art thou greater than he?"

"Adversity and affliction, when patiently borne," purify the heart, broaden the mind, and make the soul more tender and charitable. Without a sense of suffering there could be no such thing as philanthrophy, no such thing as charity."

*—Excerpts from a sermon given by Orson F. Whitney.*

## THE WORLD IS MINE

Today upon a bus, I saw a lovely maid with golden hair;

I envied her—she seemed so gay—and I wished I were as fair.

When suddenly she rose to leave, I saw her hob-
    ble down the aisle;
She had one foot and wore a crutch, but as she
    passed, a smile.
    Oh, God, forgive me when I whine;
    I have two feet—the world is mine!
And then I stopped to buy some sweets. The lad
    who sold them had such charm.
I talked with him—he said to me:
"It's nice to talk with folks like you.
"You see," he said, "I'm blind."
    Oh, God, forgive me when I whine;
    I have two eyes—the world is mine!
Then walking down the street, I saw a child with
    eyes of blue.
He stood and watched the others play;
It seemed he knew not what to do.
I stopped for a moment, then I said:
"Why don't you join the others, dear?"
He looked ahead without a word, and then
I knew, he could not hear.
    Oh, God, forgive me when I whine;
    I have two ears—the world is mine!
With feet to take me where I'd go,
With eyes to see the sunset's glow,
With ears to hear what I would know,
    Oh, God, forgive me when I whine;
    I'm blessed, indeed! The World Is Mine!

*—Author Unknown*

# COURAGE

Hungering and striving after knowledge is what makes a scholar; hungering and striving after virtue is what makes a Saint; hungering and striving after noble action is what makes a hero and a man.

*—Orison Swett Marden*

———

When you get into a tight place, and everything goes against you, 'til it seems as if you couldn't hold on a minute longer, never give up then, for that's just the place and time that the tide'll turn.

*—Harriet Beecher Stowe*

———

You cannot scare a man who is at peace with God, his fellow men, and himself. There is no room for fear in such a man's heart. When fear finds a welcome, there is something that needs awakening.

*—Napoleon Hill*

———

The lives of truest heroism are those in which there are no great deeds to look back upon. It is the little things well done that go to make up a successful and truly good life.

*—Theodore Roosevelt*

He who loses wealth loses much; he who loses a friend loses more; but he that loses his courage loses all.

*—Cervantes*

----

No one would ever have crossed the ocean if he could have gotten off the ship in a storm.

*—Anon*

----

One resolution I have made, and try always to keep, is this: To rise above little things.

*—John Burroughs*

----

Cowards die many times before their deaths; the valiant never taste of death but once.

*—Shakespeare*

----

Always do what you are afraid to do.

*—Emerson*

----

## THE LAW OF LIFE

The tree that never had to fight
For sun and sky and air and light,
That stood out in the open plain,
And always got its share of rain,
Never became a forest king.

The man who never had to toil,
Who never had to win his share,
Of sun and sky and light and air,
Never became a manly man,
But lived and died as he began.

Good timber does not grow in ease;
The stronger wind, the tougher trees;
The more the storm, the more the
    strength;
By sun and cold, by rain and snow,
In tree or man, good timber grows.

Where thickest stands the forest growth,
We find the patriarchs of both,
And they hold converse with the stars,
Whose broken branches show the scars
Of many winds and much of strife.
This is the common law of life.

—*Author Unknown*

---

The real acid test of courage is to be just your honest self when everybody is trying to be like somebody else.

—*Andrew Jensen*

---

Jesus gave thirty years preparation for less than three years' work. Do you wonder that his work lasts? Moses was eighty years in the tanner's pit of preparation. Is it strange that his life wears to this day? The Apostle Paul devoted three years to solitary meditation in the Arabian desert before he began his Christian work. Does not that account for the enduring influence of his epistles? The gospel of John was fashioned after more than half a century of Christian experience and service, and even the critics cannot break it or wear it out.

*—George Henry Hubbard*

## TODAY

With every rising of the sun
Think of your life as just begun.

The past has cancelled and buried deep
All yesterdays. There let them sleep.

Concern yourself with but today;
Grasp it, and teach it to obey.

You and today! A soul sublime
And the great heritage of time.
With God himself to find the twain
Go forth, brave heart! Attain! Attain!

*—Author Unknown*

## ONWARD

Keep the onward look.
Keep your eyes ever and always toward the
    horizon,

When all about you there is confusion, chaos,
    frustration, barriers—all doors seem shut,
And there is no fulfilment to your need,
No solvent to your problem . . .
You feel so utterly alone and lonely,
With no one to help whatever,
And it seems even that no one cares—
You cannot, you must not
Quit faith.

These things will change just as the night
    changes to the day.
This present will another day become a past.
This present may not hold the elements of
    fulfilment for you now—but never mind,
Just don't look at it now, look away;
Look above it, beyond it, look beyond the moun-
    taintop, even.
Look toward the horizon—for there shall
    be new dawning in your world, in your life,
    as surely as there follows after every flam-
    ing sunset a golden sunrise.

There will be for you: harmony, fulfilment,
    love, peace, success.
Keep the onward look.
The now is a period of waiting, of patience,
    of deepening understanding.
Each cycle has its own time and hour—and
    that other time and hour shall come as surely
    as springtime ripens into summer.

Keep your heart filled with this knowing, this
    comfort, this courage.
The fulfilment hour is ahead—it is on the way.
Give it a little more time ...
Keep the onward look.

—*Virginia Stillman*

———

## TRIUMPH

If you can sing,
When there is no song in your heart;
If you can keep on being loving, lovable, and
    lovely,
When those who should be loving you are blind;
If you can hold a lifted brow,
Despite the weights your shoulders cannot
    bear—
There is benediction there
For you to share.

If you can carry on dry-eyed
While your heart is drowning
In a deluge of tears;
If you can keep on going,
When the pain in you is just too great,
And your soul is shaken with hopeless anguish,
And your suffering, ache-filled body wants to
    slump;
If you can keep on going—
And keep on going ...

When nerves and blood and muscle scream and
    sob
With the injustice and unholy ways
Of those who should be warm and just, but
    can't be,
Because the abysmal holds for them more lure
Than the celestial—
Why, God?

But, if you can tilt your cheeks, sunward,
Keeping your eyes filled with spiritual light
    and message,
And coax a skip of childlike rhythm
Into your lagging walk—
And lift your best foot forward,
As though you had no care—
There is benediction there
For you to share.

                  *—Virginia Stillman*

—————

> *Four things come not back,*
> *The spoken word,*
> *The sped arrow,*
> *The past life,*
> *The neglected opportunity.*
>
>         *—Arabian Proverb*

# DAILY INVENTORY

When evening comes, go off into a quiet place and review your day.

Have you been kind and thoughtful, or mean and thoughtless?

Have you kept an even temper, or have you lost your temper when things have gone wrong?

Have you been pleasant, or grouchy?

Have you inspired those whom you have met, or have you depressed and discouraged them?

Have you done something creative and worth while, or have you wasted the day with petty things?

Have you been square and fair in what you've done?

Have you increased the happiness-moments in the lives of others, or have you thought only of self?

Have you enlarged your mental horizon, expanded your personality—have you grown larger, or shrunk smaller?

What we do day by day determines what we become. Hour by hour we build our lives for better or for worse. A daily inventory will help to keep us on the right track, headed toward our highest ideals.

*—The Silver Lining*

# DEATH

I am standing upon the seashore; a ship at my side spreads her white sails to the morning breeze and starts for the blue ocean.

She is an object of beauty and strength, and I stand and watch her until—at length—she hangs like a speck of white cloud just where the sea and sky come down to mingle with each other.

Then someone at my side says, "There! She's gone." Gone where? Gone from my sight—that is all.

She is just as large in mast and hull and spar as she was when she left my side and just as able to bear her load of living freight to the place of destination.

Her diminished size is in me, not in her; and just as the moment when someone at my side says, "There! She's gone," there are other eyes watching her coming and other voices ready to take up the glad shout, "There she comes!"

And that is dying.

*—Author Unknown*

## DEATH IS LIKE SLEEP

As a fond mother, when the day is o'er
    Leads by the hand her little child to bed,
    Half-willing, half-reluctant to be led
    And leaves his broken playthings on the floor

Still gazing at them through the open door,
    Nor wholly reassured and comforted
    By promises of others in their stead,
    Which, though more splendid, may not please
    him more;

So nature deals with us, and takes away
    Our playthings one by one, and by the hand
    Leads us to rest so gently, that we go

Scarce knowing if we wish to go or stay,
    Being too full of sleep to understand
    How far the unknown transcends the what
    we know.

*—Longfellow*

There is no flock, however watched and tended,
    But one dead lamb is there!
There is no fireside, howsoe'er defended,
    But has one vacant chair!

*—Longfellow*

——oOo——

# EXAMPLE

## MYSELF

I have to live with myself, and so
I want to be fit for myself to know;
I want to be able as days go by
Always to look myself straight in the eye;
I don't want to stand with the setting sun
And hate myself for the things I've done.

I don't want to keep on a closet shelf
A lot of secrets about myself,
And fool myself as I come and go
Into thinking nobody else will know
The kind of man I really am;
I don't want to dress me up in sham.

I want to go out with my head erect,
I want to deserve all men's respect;
But here in the struggle for fame and pelf,
I want to be able to like myself.
I don't want to think as I come and go
That I'm bluster and bluff and empty show.

I can never hide myself from me,
I see what others can never see,
I know what others may never know—
I never can fool myself—and so,
Whatever happens, I want to be
Self-respecting and conscience-free.

—*Edgar A. Guest*

## SERMONS WE SEE

I'd rather see a sermon than hear one any day;
I'd rather one should walk with me than merely
show the way.
The eye's a better pupil and more willing than
the ear;
Fine counseling is confusing, but example's always clear.

And the best of all the preachers are the men
 who live their creeds,
For to see the good in action is what everybody
 needs.
I can soon learn how to do it if you'll let me see
 it done;
I can watch your hands in action, but your
 tongue too fast may run.

And the lectures you deliver may be very wise
 and true,
But I'd rather get my lesson by observing what
 you do;
For I may misunderstand you and the high advice you give,
But there's no misunderstanding how you act
 and how you live.

        —*Edgar A. Guest*

———

What you are thunders so loudly in my ears
that I cannot hear what you say.

         —*Anon.*

———

## THE MEASURE OF MAN

 Not—
  "How did he die?"
 But—
  "How did he live?"

Not—
  "What did he gain?"
But—
    "What did he give?"

These are the units
  To measure the worth
Of a man, as a man,
  Regardless of birth.

Not—
  "What was his station?"
But—
  "Had he a heart?"
And—
  "How did he play
  His god-given part?"

Was he ever ready
  With a word of good cheer,
To bring back a smile,
  To banish a tear?"

Not—
  "What was his church?"
Nor—
  "What was his creed?"
But—
  "Had he befriended
  Those really in need?"

Not—
  "What did the sketch
  In the newspaper say?"
But—
  "How many were sorry
  When he passed away?"

—Kansas City *Star*

## A BRIEF DESCRIPTION OF
## A BRIEF LIFE

Here is a man who was born in an obscure village, child of a peasant woman. He grew up in another obscure village. He worked in a carpenter shop until he was thirty, and then for three years he was an itinerant preacher. He never wrote a book. He never held an office. He never owned a home. He never had a family. He never went to college. He never put his foot inside a big city. He never traveled two hundred miles from the place where he was born. He never did one of the things that usually accompany greatness. He had no credentials but himself. He had nothing to go with this world except the naked power of his divine manhood.

While he was still a young man, the tide of popular opinion turned against him. His friends ran away. One of them denied him. Another betrayed him. One of them turned him over to his enemies. He went through the mockery of a trial. He was nailed upon the cross between two thieves. His executioners gambled for the only piece of property he had on earth while he was dying and that was his coat. When he was dead, he was taken down and laid in a borrowed grave through the pity of a friend.

Nineteen wide centuries have come and gone, and today he is the center of the human race and the leader of the column of progress.

I am far within the mark when I say that all the armies that ever marched, and all the navies that were ever built, and all the parliaments that ever sat, and all the kings that ever reigned, put together, have not affected the life of man upon this earth as powerfully as this one solitary life.

—James Allan Francis

# ENEMIES

## NO ENEMIES

You have no enemy, you say?
Alas, friend, the boast is poor;
He who hath mingled in the fray
Of duty, that the brave endure,
Must have made foes! If you have none,
Small is the work that you have done.

You've hit no traitor on the hip,
You've dashed no cup from perjured lip,
You've never turned the wrong to right,
You've been a coward in the fight.

*—Charles Mackay.*

I never see a person trying to disclose
The scarlet letter on another's breast
That I do not wonder if he doesn't carry
Some mark of disgrace, which would ruin
Him, had he been overtaken by justice.

*—Napoleon Hill.*

# FAILURE

There are ten weaknesses against which most of us must guard ourselves. One of these is the habit of trying to reap before we have sown, and the other nine are all wrapped up in the one practice of creating alibis to cover every mistake made.

*—Napoleon Hill.*

Edison failed 10,000 times before he made the electric light. Do not be discouraged if you fail a few times.

*—Napoleon Hill.*

It is hard to fail, but it is worse never to have tried to succeed.

*—Theodore Roosevelt.*

Never give a man up until he has failed at something he likes.

—*Lewis E. Lawes.*

Christianity hasn't failed—It hasn't been tried.

—*Anon.*

Not failure but low aim is crime.

—*James Russell Lowell.*

——oOo——

# FRIENDSHIP

The only way to have a friend is to be one. A friend is a person with whom I may be sincere. Before him I may think aloud. Happy is the house that shelters a friend. A friend may well be reckoned the masterpiece of nature. Let the soul be assured that somewhere in the universe it should rejoin its friend, and it would be content and cheerful alone for a thousand years.

—*Ralph Waldo Emerson.*

———

One tends to become like his friends and to be judged by them. Avoid attaching to yourself as friends persons who are intemperate, avaricious, extravagant, or ungrateful.

—*Joy Elmer Morgan.*

Go often to the house of thy friend, for weeds choke up the unused path.

—*Shakespeare.*

---

Friends are an aid to the young, to guard them from error; to the elderly, to attend to their wants, and to supplement their failing power of action; to those in the prime of life, to assist them to noble deeds.

—*Aristotle.*

---

If a man does not make new acquaintances as he advances through life, he will soon find himself alone; one should keep his friendships in constant repair.

—*Johnson.*

---

Tell me with whom thou art found, and I will tell thee who thou art.

—*Goethe.*

---

It is not when riches or splendor surround us
　　That friendship and friends can be put to the
　　　test;
'Tis but when affliction's cold presence hath
　　bound us,
　　We find which the hearts are that love us the
　　　best,

For friends will fawn
At fortune's dawn,
When the breeze and the tide bear us steadily
on;
But when sorrow o'ertake us,
Each false one forsakes us,
And leaves us to sink and to struggle alone.

*—Anon.*

———

## A VANISHED FRIEND

Around the corner I have a friend
In this great city that has no end;
Yet days go by and weeks rush on,
And before I know it a year is gone,
And I never see my old friend's face,
For life is a swift and terrible race.
He knows I like him just as well
As in the days when I rang his bell
And he rang mine. We were younger then,
And now we are busy, tired men—
Tired with playing a foolish game,
Tired with trying to make a name.

"Tomorrow," I say, "I will call on Jim,
Just to show that I'm thinking of him."
But tomorrow comes—and tomorrow goes,
And the distance between us grows and
grows,
Around the corner!—yet miles away . . .

"Here's a telegram, sir" . . . "Jim died
   today!"
And that's what we get, and deserve in the
   end—
Around the corner, a vanished friend.

—*Charles Hanson Towne*

——oOo——

# FAITH AND WORKS

James Hart and the late J. Golden Kimball
fell in love with the same girl. Golden Kimball
was truly concerned and took up the matter
with one of the church authorities.

It was suggested that he fast and pray.

Some months later Golden met the authority
who had advised him, and the latter inquired
about his affairs. Golden replied, "While I was
home fasting and praying, James Hart married
the girl."

The authority said, "That just proves to us
all that faith without works is dead."

———

A certain brother purchased a run-down farm
and made it blossom as the rose.

One day he desired the minister to come and
see it.

The minister was greatly astonished and said, "My, what wonders you and the Lord have accomplished."

To this comment the brother replied, "But you should have seen it when the Lord was working it alone."

———oOo———

# GIVING

## UNAWARES

They say the Master is coming
To honor the town today,
And none can tell at whose house or
    home
The Master will choose to stay.
And I thought while my heart beat
    wildly,
What if he should come to mine?
How would I strive to entertain
And honor this Guest Divine?

And straight I turned to toiling,
To make my house more neat;
I swept and polished and garnished,
And decked it with blossoms sweet,
I was troubled for fear the Master
Might come ere my task was done,
And hastened and worked the faster
And watched the hurrying sun.

But right in the midst of my duties
A woman came to my door;
She had come to tell me her sorrows,
And my comfort and aid implore.
And I said, "I cannot listen,
Nor help you any today;
I have greater things to attend to,"
And the pleader turned away.

But soon there came another—
A cripple, thin, pale, and gray—
And said, O, let me stop and rest
Awhile in your home, I pray.
I have traveled far since morning,
I am hungry, and faint and weak
My heart is full of misery,
And comfort and help I seek."

And I said, "I am grieved and sorry
But I cannot help you today;
I look for the great and noble guest."
And the cripple went away.
The day wore onward swiftly
And my task was nearly done,
And a prayer was ever in my heart,
That the Master to me might come.

And I thought I would spring to meet
    him,
And serve him with utmost care,
When a little child stood by me
With a face so sweet and fair—

Sweet, but with marks of tear drops
And his clothes were tattered and old;
A finger was bruised and bleeding,
And his little bare feet were cold.

And I said, "I'm sorry for you,
You are sorely in need of care;
But I cannot stop to give it,
You must hasten on elsewhere."
And at the words a shadow
Swept o'er his blue-veined brow—
"Someone will feed and clothe you, dear,
But I am too busy now."

At last the day was ended
And my toil was over and done
My house was swept and garnished,
And I watched in the dark alone;
Watched, but no footsteps sounded,
No one e'er paused at the gate,
No one entered my cottage door,
I could only pause and wait.

I waited until night had deepened,
And the Master had not come;
"He has entered some other door," I
    cried,
"And gladdened some other home,
My labor has been for nothing."
And I bowed my head and I wept,
My heart was sore with longing,
Yet in spite of all I slept.

Then the Master stood before me.
His face was grave and fair;
"Three time today I came to your
    door,
And craved your pity and care;
Three times you sent me onward,
Unhelped and uncomforted,
And the blessings you might have had
    are lost,
And your chance to serve has fled."

"Oh, Lord, dear Lord, forgive me
How could I know it was Thee?"
My very soul was shamed and bowed
In the depths of humility.
And he said, "The sin is pardoned
But the blessing is lost to thee;
For comforting not the least of mine,
You have failed to comfort me."

*Author Unknown.*

———

## TWO SEAS

There are two seas in Palestine. One is fresh
and fish are in it. Splashes of green adorn its
banks. Trees spread their branches over it and
spread their thirsty roots to sip its healing
waters. Along its shores the children play, as
children played when he was there. He loved

it. He could look across its silvery surface when he spoke his parables, and on a rolling plain not far away he fed the five thousand people.

The river Jordan makes this sea with sparkling water from the hill, so it laughs in the sunshine. Men build their houses near it, and birds build their nests there. Every kind of life is happier because it is there.

This river Jordan flows farther on south into another sea. Here are no splashing of fish, no fluttering leaf, no song of birds, no children's laughter. Travelers choose another route when passing. The air hangs heavy above its waters, that neither man nor beast nor fowl will drink.

What makes this mighty difference in these neighboring seas? Not the soil in which they lie, nor the country roundabout. The sea of Galilee receives but does not keep the Jordan. For every drop that flows into it, another flows out. The giving and receiving go on in equal measure.

The other sea is shrewder, hoarding its income jealously. It will not be tempted into generous impulse. Every drop it gets it keeps. Receiving all and giving nothing—it is called "The Dead Sea." The other sea gives and lives.

There are two seas in Palestine; and two kinds of people in the world.

—*Bruce Barton.*

## GIVING

He who giveth receiveth!

And now, if God, who has created you, on whom you are dependent for your lives and for all that ye have and are, doth grant unto you whatsoever ye ask that is right, in faith, believing that ye shall receive, O then, how ye ought to impart of the substance, that we have one to another.

*—Mosiah* 4.

---

## THE MISER

A Miser once buried all his money in the earth, at the foot of a tree, and went every day to feast upon the sight of his treasure. A thievish fellow, who had watched him at this occupation, came one night and carried off the gold. The next day the miser, finding his treasure gone, tore his clothes and filled the air with his lamentations.

A neighbor hearing his outcry and learning the cause said, "Pray do not grieve so; but go and get a stone, place it in the hole, and fancy it is your gold. It will be of quite as much service as the money was."

Nothing is of value that is not of use.

Many a preacher has lost his flock because he insisted on giving a quart when they could only hold a pint.

A minister prepared a splendid sermon but when the day to deliver it came, he found but one lone rancher in t h e audience. Doubtful about giving his sermon to just one, the minister discussed it with the rancher. The rancher said, "Well, I ain't educated, but if I had a load of hay, and there was only one hungry cow, I believe I'd give it the hay." The minister proceeded w i t h his sermon. After an hour's discourse, the minister looked at his friend and found him asleep. He awakened him and inquired if he should continue his sermon. The rancher drawled, "I don't know much, but if I had a whole load of hay and one cow, I don't think I'd give it the whole load."

———

A Baptist minister was guest at the Presbyterian church. He delivered a powerful sermon. When the collection box was passed, he set the example and contributed first. After it was passed around, it was returned to him.

He looked chagrined as he withdrew his own fifty cent piece, the only coin in the tray.

A little lad on the first row observed the disappointed look and cried, "Mister, if you had put more in, you would have taken more out."

If you want to be miserable, think about yourself, about what you want, what y o u like, what respect people ought to pay you, and then nothing to you will be pure. You will spoil everything you touch, you will make misery for yourself out of everything which God sends you. You will be as wretched as you choose.

—*Charles Kingsley.*

———oOo———

# GOODNESS

What makes a saint?

Why were the saints, saints?

Because they were cheerful when it w a s difficult to be cheerful; patient when it was difficult to be patient; and because they pushed on when they wanted to stand still; and kept silent when they wanted to talk; a n d were agreeable when they wanted to be disagreeable.

That was all!

It was quite simple and always will be.

—*Personal Growth Leaflet.*

———

We live in deed, not years; in thoughts, not breaths; in feelings, not in figures on a dial. We should count time by heartthrobs. He most lives who thinks most, feels the noblest, acts the best.

—*Philip James Bailey.*

———

A good deed is never lost. He who sows courtesy, reaps friendship; he who plants kindness, gathers love; pleasure bestowed upon a grateful mind was never sterile, but generally gratitude begets reward.

—*Basil.*

———

Do all the good you can, in all the ways you can, to all the souls you can, in every place you can, at all times you can, with all the zeal you can, as long as ever you can.

*J. Wesley.*

———

Die when I may, I want it said of me by those who knew me best, that I always plucked a thistle and planted a flower where I thought a flower would grow.

—*Abraham Lincoln.*

———

Great minds, like heaven, are pleased in doing good, though the ungrateful subjects of their favors are barren in return.

—*Rowe.*

There never was a day that did not bring its own opportunity for doing good, that never could have been done before, and never can be again.

*W. H. Burleigh.*

———

Trifles make perfection, but perfection is no trifle.

*—Michelangelo*

———

He who wants to do a great deal of good at once will never do anything. Life is made up of little things. It is very rarely that an occasion is offered for doing a great deal at once. True greatness consists in being great in little things.

*—C. Simmons*

———

They that know no evil will suspect none.

*—Ben Johnson.*

———

When a person is down in the world, an ounce of help is better than a pound of preaching.

*—Bulwer Lytton.*

———

Most of us will do anything to become good except change our way of living.

*—Anon.*

We do not count a man's years until he has nothing else to count.

—*Anon.*

———

There never was yet a truly great man that was not at the same time truly virtuous.

—*Franklin.*

———

A good name is rather to be chosen than great riches, and loving favor than silver and gold.

—*Proverbs* 21:1

———

A horse can't pull while kicking,
This fact I merely mention;
And he can't kick while pulling,
Which is my chief contention.

Let's imitate the good old horse
And lead a life that's fitting.
Just pull an honest load and then
There'll be no time for kicking.

—*Author Unknown.*

———

### TODAY'S THOUGHT

The ones who seek their happiness
By buying cars and clothes and rings,
Don't seem to know that empty lives
Are just as empty filled with things.

—*Anon.*

# HAPPINESS

Happiness is not the end of life; character is.
—*H. W. Beecher*.

---

Happiness consists of having three things: Someone to love, work to do, and a clear conscience.
—*Anon*.

---

The highest pinnacle of spiritual life is not happy joy in unbroken sunshine, but absolute and undoubting trust in the love of God.
—*Anon*.

---

No thoroughly occupied man was ever very miserable.
—*L. E. Landon*.

---

## TWELVE RULES FOR HAPPINESS

Happiness is a habit—a by-product of right thinking and living. Here are twelve rules for happiness:

1. Live a simple life. Be temperate in your habits. Avoid self-seeking and selfishness. Make simplicity the keynote of your daily plans. Simple things are best.

2. Spend less than you earn. This may be difficult, but it pays large dividends in contentment. Keep out of debt. Cultivate frugality, prudence, and self-denial. Avoid extravagance.

3. Think constructively. Train yourself to think clearly and accurately. Store your mind with useful thought. Stand guard at the door of your mind.

4. Cultivate a yielding disposition. Resist the common tendency to want things your own way. See the other person's viewpoint.

5. Be grateful. Begin the day with gratitude for your opportunities and blessings. Be glad for the privilege of life and work.

6. Rule your moods. Cultivate a mental attitude of peace and good will.

7. Give generously. There is no greater joy in life than to render happiness to others by means of intelligent giving.

8. Work with right motives. The highest purpose of your life should be to grow in spiritual grace and power.

9. Be interested in others. Divert your mind from self-centeredness. To the degree that you give, serve, and help, you will experience the by-product of happiness.

10. Live in a "day-tight" compartment. That

is, live one day at a time. Concentrate on your immediate task. Make the most of today.

11. Have a hobby! Nature study, walking, gardening, music, golfing, carpentry, stamp collecting, sketching, voice culture, foreign language, chess, books, photography, social service, public speaking, travel, authorship. Cultivate an avocation to which you can turn for diversion and relaxation.

12. Keep close to God. True and enduring happiness depends primarily upon close alliance with him. It is your privilege to share his thoughts for your spiritual nourishment and to have constant assurance of divine protection and guidance.

—*Grenville Kleiser.*

---

## YOUR HOUSE OF HAPPINESS

Take what God gives, O heart of mine,
And build your house of happiness.
Perchance some have been given more,
But many have been given less,
The treasures lying at your feet,
The value you but faintly guess,
Another builder looking on,
Would barter heaven to possess.

Have you found work that you can do?
Is there a heart that loves you best?

Is there a spot somewhere called home
Where, spent and worn, your soul may
    rest?
A friendly tree? A book? A song?
A dog that loves your hand's caress?
A store of health to meet life's need—
Oh, build your house of happiness.

Trust not tomorrow's dawn to bring
The dreamed of joy for which you wait,
You have enough of pleasant things
To house your soul in goodly state;
Tomorrow's time's relentless stream
May bear what now you have away.
Take what God gives, O hear, and build
Your house of happiness today.

                              —*Mrs. B. Y. Williams.*

———oOo———

# HOME

An artist desired to find the greatest thing in the world so that he could portray it on canvas. He traveled the world over in search of it. In his travels he met a philosopher and asked him what the greatest thing was. He answered, "Faith." The artist wondered how he could portray faith on canvas. He traveled farther and met a young bride whom he asked what was the greatest thing was. She answered, "Love — that encompasseth all." This again caused thought on the part of the artist, and he again wondered how to portray it on canvas. He then met a war-weary soldier and asked his opinion as to what was the greatest thing in the world. The soldier answered, "Peace." Now, again, the artist wondered how to portray this with paints and brush. Finally, after many months' search he returned to his home, feeling, probably, that his search was in vain. Upon arriving home he entered his front door. There he saw his wife and family. His children looked at him with "Faith" in their eyes; his wife smiled forth "Love," and "Peace" reigned in their midst. Here at last was the thing he had been searching. He busily began painting, and when he had completed his masterpiece, he called it "Home."

*—Anon.*

In our lives,
It is impossible for us to
Cheat a little and still
Be honest.

*—Elder Henry D. Moyle.*

——oOo——

# HONESTY

## HONEST WEIGHT

Burell Bybee of Ely tells the story of the old farmer who made a trip to town each week with farm produce which he traded to a merchant for various items he needed. One day after the farmer left the store, the merchant happened to weigh a pound of the butter he had just left. He was surprised to find it one ounce short. He quickly weighed another pound and another and found them all short exactly one ounce.

Next week when the farmer came, the merchant told him he was through doing business with him and told of his discovery about the butter. He explained that a man who would stoop so low as to make his butter and cheese one ounce short of a pound just to get a little more out of it wasn't the kind of person he cared to deal with.

The old farmer looked sad and said, "Well, we're just poor people. We don't even own a pair of scales, so in order to measure how much butter or cheese to put in a pound we rigged up a sort of balance. We set a pound of sugar or rice we've just bought from you on one side, and when the butter on the other side balances evenly, we figure it is a pound."

—*Anon.*

———

Bernard Shaw said of Honor: "You cannot believe in Honor until you have achieved it. Better keep yourself clean and bright: You are the window through which you must see the world."

"It is the easiest path in the world to be honest—
To be upright before God; and when people learn this,
They will practise it."

—*Brigham Young.*

———oOo———

# MANKIND

If you would really know men, study them:
When angry.
When in love.
When eating (alone and unobserved, as they believe).
When writing.
When in trouble.
When joyful and triumphant.
When downcast and defeated.
When facing catastrophe of a hazardous nature.
When trying to make a "good impression" on others.
When informed of another's misfortune.
When informed of another's good fortune.
When losing in any sort of a game of sport.
When winning at sport.
When alone, in a meditative mood.

—*Napoleon Hill.*

The broad general rule is that a man is about as big as the things that make him angry.

—*Anon.*

————oOo————

# OPPORTUNITY

This I beheld, or dreamed it in a dream:
There spread a cloud of dust along a plain;
And underneath the cloud, or in it raged
A furious battle, and men yelled, and swords
Shocked upon swords and shields. A prince's
   banner wavered, then staggered backward,
   hemmed by foes.
A craven hung along the battle's edge and
   thought,
"Had I a sword of keener steel—
That blue blade that the king's son bears—but
This blunt thing — !" He snapt and flung it
   from his hand,
And, lowering, crept away and left the field.
Then came the king's son, wounded, sore be-
   stead,
And weaponless, and saw the broken sword,
Hilt buried in the dry and trodden sand.
And ran and snatched it, and with battle-shout
Lifted afresh, he hewed his enemy down,
And saved a great cause that heroic day.

—*Edward Rowland Sill.*

Things don't turn up in this world until somebody turns them up.

—*Garfield.*

———

Rather than wait for extraordinary opportunities, we should seize common occasions and make them great as did Canova—one of the greatest sculptors of all times. The following story tells how the boy Antonio took advantage of his first opportunity which made him the famous Canova.

"If you will let me try, I think I can make something that will do," said a boy who had been employed as a scullion at the mansion of Signor Faliero, as the story is told by George Cary Eggleston. A large company had been invited to a banquet, and just before the hour the confectioner, who had been making a large ornament for the table, sent word that he had spoiled the piece. "You!" exclaimed the head servant, in astonishment; "and who are you?" "I am Antonio Canova, the grandson of Pisano, the stone-cutter," replied the pale-faced little fellow.

"And, pray, what can you do?" asked the major-domo.

"I can make you something that will do for the middle of the table, if you will let me try." The servant was at his wit's end, so he told

Antonio to go ahead and see what he could do. Calling for some butter, the scullion quickly molded a large crouching lion, which the admiring major-domo placed upon the table.

Dinner was announced, and many of the most noted merchants, princes, and noblemen of Venice were ushered into the dining room. Among them were skilled critics of art work. When their eyes fell upon the butter lion, they forgot the purpose for which they had come in their wonder at such a work of genius. They looked at the lion long and carefully, and asked Signor Faliero what great sculptor had been persuaded to waste his skill upon such a temporary material. Faliero could not tell; so he asked the head servant, who brought Antonio before the company.

When the distinguished guests learned that the lion had been made in a short time by a scullion, the dinner was turned into a feast in his honor. The rich host declared that he would pay the boy's expenses under the best masters, and he kept his word. Antonio was not spoiled by his good fortune but remained at heart the same simple, earnest, faithful boy who had tried so hard to become a good stonecutter in the shop of Pisano."

Weak men wait for opportunities, strong men make them.

—*Orison Swett Marden.*

Wise men are instructed in reason
Men of less understanding by experience,
The most unknowing learn by necessity
Wise men do in the beginning what
    fools do
In the end.               *—Anon.*

———oOo———

# BITS OF PHILOSOPHY
## MODERN PHILOSOPHY

Did it ever occur to you that a man's life is full of crosses and temptations? He comes into this world without his consent, and goes out against his will, and the trip is exceedingly rocky. The rule of the contraries is one of the important features of the trip.

When he is little, the big girls kiss him; when he is big, the little girls kiss him.

If he is poor, he is a bad manager; if he is rich, he is dishonest.

If he needs credit, he can't get it; if he is prosperous, everyone wants to do him a favor.

If he is in politics, it is for graft, if he is out of politics, he is not good for his country.

If he doesn't give to charity, he is a tightwad; if he does, it is for show.

If he is actively religious, he is a hypocrite;

if he takes no part in religion, he is a hardened sinner.

If he shows affection, he is a soft specimen; if he cares for no one, he is cold-blooded.

If he dies young, there was a great future before him; if he lives to an old age, he missed his calling.

The road is a rocky one, but men love to travel it.

—*Anon.*

———

Look for the best, prepare for the worst, and take what comes.

—*Anon.*

———

A good citizen upon learning that his friend was ill paid him a visit. The sick man complained bitterly about his fate. "Everything happens to me," he said. "First my cow gets tuberculosis, then my barn burns down, and now I have lumbago."

The friend, trying to cheer him, said, "It could be worse." To each complaint, he kept saying, "But it could be worse." Finally, in exasperation, the sick man exclaimed, "How could it be worse?" The friend replied, "It could have happened to me."

## A MAN AND HIS TWO WIVES

In a country where Man could have more than one Wife, a certain Man, whose head was fast becoming white, had two, one a little older than himself, and one m u c h younger. The young Wife, being of a gay and lively turn, did not want people to think that she had an old man for a husband, and so used to pull out as many of his white hairs as she could. The old Wife, on the other hand, did not wish to seem older than her husband, and so used to pull out the black hairs. This went on, until between them both, they made the poor Man quite bald.

Those who seek to please everybody, end by pleasing nobody.

———

## CHEESE AND CRACKERS

Once I heard a speaker tell the following story: A certain woman had long wanted to take a cruise and had saved her money to that end. Finally the day came when she was able to purchase a ticket for the much-desired voyage.

As she carefully planned for the trip, she said to herself,

"Of course it would be wonderful to eat in the dining room on the boat. I won't have money enough to eat all meals there, but I can take some cheese and crackers along for the first part of the trip, and then I can go to the dining room for the last meal. I'll have money enough for one meal on the boat."

In high spirits the good woman set out for the thrilling experience of her first water trip. At mealtime, after wistfully watching the other passengers file into the dining room, she would go off into some corner and eat her cheese and crackers, trying all the while not to be envious.

Then the last day arrived, and time for the final meal aboard ship. She went in with the other passengers "to eat in style," as she put it.

It was one of life's big moments for her, and she lingered long to enjoy it. When she had at last finished the meal, she sat patiently waiting for her check, but when none was presented to her, she beckoned the waiter and asked for it.

"Let me see your ticket, madam," said the waiter, and when she handed it to him, he gave it back with, "Madam, all your meals were included in the price of the ticket."

Of that woman, without hesitation, we say: "How stupid! Why didn't she l o o k at her ticket? Or why didn't some other passenger tell her she could eat on the boat?" But of ourselves what do we say?

Are we not all passengers on God's big universal ocean liner? In our ignorance of what our ticket includes, do we, like the woman in the story, eat "cheese and crackers"?

"Come, for all things now are ready."

"It is your Father's good pleasure to give you the kingdom."

"Hitherto have ye asked nothing. . . . Ask, and ye shall receive, that your joy may be made full."

"Eye hath not seen, nor ear heard, neither have entered into the heart of man, the things which God hath prepared for them that love him."

And yet we do stick to "the cheese and crackers!"

—*Grace A. Thompson.*

---

## "THIS, TOO, SHALL PASS AWAY"

When sorrows come into your life
  And threaten to destroy
The very things you treasure most,
  Your happiness and joy;
And when that crushing power
  Threatens everything worth while,
And clouds of darkness gather
  And you find it hard to smile;
Then lift your head and let the world

Hear every word you say.
With faith undaunted say to them;
"This too, shall pass away."

When you are over-burdened
  With life's toil and earthly care;
When life becomes so dreary
  It seems more than you can bear;
When weariness o'ercomes you
  And you yearn for peaceful rest,
And trials of the day leave you
  Discouraged and depressed;
There is no song within your heart;
  You feel you cannot pray;
Then turn your thoughts to gladness for
  "This too, shall pass away."

When fortune smiles upon you,
  And your cup of joy is full;
When everything you want is yours,
  And life seems wonderful;
When days and weeks go flitting by
  With happiness replete;
And you desire nothing more
  To make your life complete;
Beware lest all these treasures
  Of this earth lead you astray,
And hear again these truthful words:
  "This too, shall pass away."

And so remember well these words,
  Whate'er your lot may be,

For life is ever changing—
  With such rapidity.
Our gladness turns to sadness
  When the sunshine disappears,
And sorrows change to happiness
  When God has calmed our fears.
Compared with all eternity,
  This life is but one day.
We cling to life, and yet we know
  "This too, shall pass away.

—*H. L. Frisby.*

## PHILOSOPHY

It is better to be clean than clever. You are a real Saint if you feel just a little ashamed of your very fine clothes, when you see your neighbor in rags.

The worst thing you know about yourself is the best thing to remember about yourself; it will save on your hat bill.

—*Nephi Jensen.*

A ninety-seven-year-old man when asked the secret of his youth replied, "I make the most of life as it comes, and the least of life as it goes."

—*Anon.*

# PRAYER

Many of us lose confidence in prayer because we do not realize the answer.

We ask for strength, and God sends us difficulties which make us strong.

We pray for wisdom, and God sends us problems the solution of which develops wisdom.

We plead for prosperity, and God gives us brain and brawn to work.

We plead for courage, and God gives us dangers to overcome.

We ask for favors, and God gives us opportunities.

—*Author Unknown.*

———

## HERCULES AND THE WAGONER

As a wagoner was driving his team through a miry lane, the wheels stuck fast in the clay, and the horses could get on no farther. The Man dropped on his knees, and began crying and praying to Hercules with all his might to come and help him.

"Lazy fellow!" said Hercules, "get up and stir yourself. Whip your horses stoutly, and put your shoulder to the wheel. If you want my help then, you shall have it."

Heaven helps those who help themselves.

# PRAYER

Pray often. Pray sincerely.

Have you ever knelt down to pray, and after addressing Deity, wonderel if you had turned off the light, wound up the clock, made a certain phone call? Well, stop right there because your mind is too cluttered with earthly things to converse with God.

Get up, check your light, make your phone call, wind the clock, and then kneel again in humility, when ready, and have a heart-to-heart talk with your Father in heaven.

# PRETENSE

## YOU TELL ON YOURSELF

You tell on yourself by the friends you
    seek,
By the very manner in which you speak,
By the way you employ your leisure time,
By the use you make of your dollar and
    dime;

You tell what you are by the things you
    wear,
By the spirit in which you your burdens
    bear,
By the kind of things at which you laugh,
By the records you play on the phonograph.
You tell what you are by the way you walk,
By the things of which you delight to talk,
By the manner in which you bear defeat,
By so simple a thing as the way you eat.
By the books you choose from the well-
    filled shelf;
So there's really no particle of sense
In an effort to keep up false pretense.

                              *—Anon.*

Think twice before you speak, because
    your words
And influence will plant the seed of
    either
Success or failure in the mind of
    another.

                       *—Napoleon Hill.*

# PRIDE

For me the road of life
Has been a stormy one;
Yet I have gained the
Heights, of success, alone—

Unaided, save for
Courage all my own.
Mixed were the feelings
Of exaltation, for power and
Wealth were at my command,
Secure and invulnerable I thought.
Then I chanced to look below,
And there I saw the kindly
Faces of a hundred forgotten
Friends, who had helped me
On my way.
Silence and humility mellowed
My tempered pride.

—Carl A. Barrett.

————oOo————

# SCATTER SUNSHINE

## UNINSTRUCTED

"I'm going to send you down to earth,"
  Said God to me one day,
"I'm giving you what men call 'birth'—
  Tonight you'll start away;
I want you to live with men
  Until I call you back again."

I trembled as I heard him speak,
  Yet knew that I must go;
I felt his hand upon my cheek,
  And wished that I might know—

Just what on earth would be my task,
  And timidly I dared to ask.

"Tell me before I start away
  What thou would have me do;
What message would thou have me say?
  When shall my work be through?
That I may serve thee on the earth,
  Tell me the purpose of my birth."

God smiled at me and softly said:
  "Oh, you shall find your task.
I want you free life's paths to tread,
  So do not stay to ask.
Remember, if your best you do,
  That I shall ask no more of you."

How often as my work I do,
  So commonplace and grim,
I sit and sigh and wish I knew
  If I am pleasing him.
I wonder if, with every test
  I've truly tried to do my best.

*—Edgar A. Guest.*

## THE PURPOSE OF LIFE

If you've never made another
  Have a happier time in life;
If you've never helped a brother
  Through his struggle and his strife;

If you've never been a comfort
  To the weary and the worn—
Will you tell us what you're
      here for
  In this lovely land of morn?

If you"ve never made the pathway
  Of some neighbor glow with sun;
If you've never brought a bubble
  To some fellow's heart with fun;

If you've never cheered a toiler
  That you tried to help along—
Will you tell us what you're here
      for
  In this lovely land of song?

If you've never made a comrade
  Feel the world a sweeter place
Because you lived within it,
  And had served it with your grace;

If you've never heard a woman
  Or a little child proclaim
A blessing on your bounty—
  You're a poor hand at the game.

——————
—*Anon.*

## WHICH ARE YOU?

There are two kinds of people on earth today;
Just two kinds of people, no more, I say.

Not the sinner and saint, for it's well understood,

The good are half bad, and the bad are half
    good.

Not the rich and the poor, for to rate a man's
    wealth,
You must first know the state of his conscience
    and health.

Not the humble and proud, for in life's little
    span,
Who puts on vain airs, is not counted a man.

Not the happy and sad, for the swift flying
    years
Bring each man his laughter and each man
    his tears.

No, the two kinds of people on earth I mean,
Are the people who lift, and the people who
    lean.

Wherever you go, you will find the earth's
    masses
Are always divided in just these two classes.

And, oddly enough, you will find, too, I ween,
There's only one lifter to twenty who lean.

In which class are you? Are you easing the
    load
Of overtaxed lifters, who toil down the road?

Or are you a leaner, who lets others share
Your portion of labor and worry and care?

               —*Ella Wheeler Wilcox.*

## WORTH WHILE

It is easy enough to be pleasant
  When life flows by like a song,
But the man worth while is one who will
    smile,
  When everything goes dead wrong.
For the test of the heart is trouble,
  And it always comes with the years.
And the smile that is worth the praises
    of earth
  Is the smile that shines through tears.

It is easy enough to be prudent,
  When nothing tempts you to stray,
When without or within no voice of sin,
  Is luring your soul away;
But it is only a negative virtue
  Until it is tried by fire,
And the life that is worth the honor of
    earth
  Is the one that resists desire.

By the cynic, the sad, the fallen,
  Who had no strength for the strife,
The world's highway is cumbered today;
  They make up the sum of life.
But the virtue that conquers passion,
  And the sorrow that hides a smile,
It is these that are worth the homage on
    earth
  For we find them but once in awhile.

—*Ella Wheeler Wilcox.*

## OPTIMISM

Talk happiness. The world is sad enough
Without your woes. No path is wholly rough;
Look for the places that are smooth and clear,
And speak of those, to rest the weary ear
Of Earth, so hurt by one continuous strain
Of human discontent and grief and pain.

Talk faith. The world is better off without
Your uttered ignorance and morbid doubt.
If you have faith in God, or man, or self,
Say so. If not, push back upon the shelf
Of silence all your thoughts, till faith shall
    come;
No one will grieve because your lips are dumb.

Talk health. The dreary, never-changing tale
Of mortal maladies is worn and stale.
You cannot charm, or interest, or please
By harping on that minor chord, disease.
Say you are well, or all is well with you,
And God shall hear your words and make them
    true.

—*Ella Wheeler Wilcox.*

## YOU CAN NEVER TELL

You can never tell when you send a word
    Like an arrow shot from a bow
By an archer blind, be it cruel or kind,
    Just where it may chance to go.

It may pierce the breast of your dearest
    friend,
    tipped with its poison or balm,
To a stranger's heart in life's great mart
    It may carry its pain or its calm.

You never can tell when you do an act
    Just what the result will be,
But with every deed you are sowing a seed,
    Though the harvest you may not see.

You never can tell what your thoughts will
    do
    In bringing you hate or love,
For thoughts are things, and their airy
    wings
    Are swifter than carrier doves.

They follow the law of the universe—
    Each thing must create its kind,
And they speed o'er the track to bring
    you back
    Whatever went out from your mind.

                  —*Ella Wheeler Wilcox.*

## LET US SMILE

The thing that goes the farthest towards making
    life worth while,
That costs the least and does the most, is just
    a pleasant smile,

The smile that bubbles from a heart that loves
    its fellow men
Will drive away the cloud of gloom and coax
    the sun again;
It's full of worth and goodness, too, with manly
    kindness blent—
It's worth a million dollars and doesn't cost a
    cent.

There is no room for sadness when we see a
    cheery smile,
It always has the same good look—it's never
    out of style—
It nerves us on to try again when failure makes
    us blue;
The dimples of encouragement are good for me
    and you.
It pays a higher interest, for it is merely
    lent—
It's worth a million dollars and doesn't cost
    a cent.

A smile comes very easy—you can wrinkle up
    with cheer
A hundred times before you can squeeze out
    a soggy tear.
It ripples out, moreover, to the heartstrings
    that will tug,
And always leaves an echo that is very like a
    hug.

So, smile away. Folks understand what by a
    smile is meant,
It's worth a million dollars and doesn't cost a
    cent.

*—Anon.*

————

# THE GRUMBLE FAMILY

There's a family nobody likes to meet,
They live, it is said, on Complaining Street,
In the city of Never-Are-Satisfied,
The river of Discontent beside.
They growl at that, and they growl at this;
Whatever comes there is something amiss;
And whether their station be high or humble,
They are known by the name of Grumble.

The weather is always too hot or too cold,
Summer and winter alike they scold;
Nothing goes right with the folks you meet
Down on that gloomy Complaining Street.
They growl at the rain, and they growl at the
    sun;
In fact, their growling is never done.
And if everything pleased them, there isn't a
    doubt
They'd growl that they'd nothing to grumble
    about!

And the worst thing is that if anyone stays
Among them too long he will learn their ways,

And before he dreams of the terrible jumble
He's adopted into the family of Grumble.
So it were wisest to keep our feet
From wandering into Grumbling Street;
And never to growl, whatever we do,
Lest we be mistaken for Grumblers too.

*—Author Unknown.*

## IF YOU WERE

If you were busy being kind,
Before you knew it, you would find
You'd soon forget to think 'twas true
That some one was unkind to you.

If you were busy being glad
And cheering people who are sad,
Although your heart might ache a bit,
You'd soon forget to notice it.

If you were busy being good
And doing just the best you could,
You'd not have to blame some man
Who's doing just the best he can.

If you were busy being right,
You'd find yourself too busy quite
To criticize your neighbor long
Because he's busy being wrong.

*—Author Unknown.*

## DON'T ENVY OTHER FOLKS

Don't think when you have troubles
  That your neighbor goes scot-free
Because he shows a smiling front
  And battles cheerfully.
No, man! He, too, has troubles,
  But herein the difference lies,
While you go idly moping round,
  The other fellow tries.

Don't envy other people;
  Maybe, if the truth you knew,
You'd find their burdens heavier far
  Than is the case with you.
Because a fellow, rain or shine,
  Can show a smiling face,
Don't think you'd have an easier time
  If you could take his place.

'Tis hope and cheery courage
  That incite one to retrieve
One's past mistakes, to start afresh,
  To dare and to achieve.
So smile, and if perchance you light
  The spark of hope anew
In some poor sad and burdened heart,
  All honor be to you.

—*Author Unknown.*

## SAY IT NOW

If you have a friend worth loving,
Love him. Yes, and let him know
That you love him, ere life's evening
Tinge his brow with sunset glow.
Why should good words ne'er be said
Of a friend—till he is dead?

If you hear a prayer that moves you
Sung by any child of song,
Praise it. Do not let the singer
Wait deserved praises long.
Why should one who thrills your heart
Lack the joy you may impart?

If you hear a prayer that moves you
By its humble, pleading tone,
Join it. Do not let the seeker
Bow before his God alone.
Why should not your brother share
The strength of "two or three" in
    prayer?

If you see the hot tears falling
From a brother's weeping eyes,
Share them. And by kindly sharing
Own our kinship in the skies.
Why should anyone be glad
When a brother's heart is sad?

If your work is made more easy
By a friendly, helping hand,

Say so. Speak out brave and truly
Ere the darkness veil the land.
Should a brother workman dear
Falter for a word of cheer?

Scatter thus your seeds of kindness
All enriching as you go—
Leave them. Trust the Harvest Giver;
He will make each seed to grow.
So until the happy end
Your life will never lack a friend.

*—Author Unknown.*

## SAY SOMETHING GOOD

Pick out the folks you like the least and watch
    'em for a while;
They never waste a kindly word, they never
    waste a smile;
They criicize their fellow men at every chance
    they get,
They never found a human just to suit their
    fancy yet.
From them I guess you'd learn some things if
    they were pointed out—
Some things that every one of us should know
    a lot about,
When some one "knocks" a brother, pass
    around the loving cup—

Say something good about him if you have to
    make it up.

It's safe to say that every man God made holds
    trace of good
That he would fain exhibit to his fellows if he
    could;
The kindly deeds in many a soul are hibernating
    there,
Awaiting the encouragement of other souls that
    dare
To show the best that's in them; and a uni-
    versal move
Would start the whole world running in a hope-
    ful, helpful groove.
Say something sweet to paralyze the "knock-
    er" on the spot—
Speak kindly of his victim if you know the
    man or not.

The eyes that peek and peer to find the worst
    a brother holds,
The tongue that speaks in bitterness, that frets
    and fumes and scolds;
The hands that bruise the fallen, though their
    strength was made to raise
The weaklings who have stumbled at the part-
    ing of the ways—
All these should be forgiven, for they "know
    not what they do";
Their hindrance makes a greater work for wiser
    ones like you.

So, when they scourge a wretched one who's
    drained sin's bitter cup,
Say something good about him if you have to
    make it up.

                    *—Anon.*

## NOW

If you have hard work to do,
    Do it now.
Today the skies are clear and blue,
Tomorrow clouds may come in view,
Yesterday is not for you;
    Do it now.

It you have a song to sing,
    Sing it now.
Let the notes of gladness ring
Clear as song of bird in spring;
Let every day some music bring;
    Sing it now.

If you have kind words to say,
    Say them now.
Tomorrow may not come your way,
Do a kindness while you may,
Loved ones will not always stay;
    Say them now.

If you have a smile to show,
    Show it now.

Make hearts happy, roses grow,
Let the friends around you know
The love you have before they go;
    Show it now.

                 —*Anon.*

## NEAR THE DAWN

When life's troubles gather darkly
    Round the way we follow here,
When no hope the sad heart lightens,
    No voice speaks a word of cheer;
Then the thought the shadow scatters,
    Giving us a cheering ray,
When the night appears the darkest,
    Morning is not far away.

When adversity surrounds us,
    And our sunshine friends pass by,
And the dreams so fondly cherished
    With our shattered treasures lie;
Then amid such gloomy seasons
    This sweet thought can yet be drawn,
When the darkest hour is present,
    It is always near the dawn.

When the spirit fluttering lingers
    On the confines of this life,
Parting from all joyful memories,
    And from every scene of strife,
Though the scene is sad and gloomy,

And the body shrinks in fear,
These dark hours will soon be vanished,
And the glorious morn be here.

Pain cannot affect us always,
    Brighter days will soon be here;
Sorrow may oppress us often,
    Yet a happier time is here;
All along our earthly journey
    This reflection lights the way,
Nature's darkest hour is always
    Just before the break of day.

—*Anon.*

## I'M GLAD I TOUCHED SHOULDERS WITH YOU

There's a comforting thought at the close of
    day,
When I am weary and lonely and sad,
That sort of grips hold of my crusty old heart,
And bids it be merry and glad.
It gets in my soul and it drives out the blues,
And finally thrills through and through.
It is just a sweet memory that chants the
    refrain:
"I'm glad I touched shoulders with you!"
Did you know you were brave, did you know
    you were strong?

Did you know that you helped when I erred?
Did you know there was one leaning hard?
Did you know that I waited and listened and
    prayed?
And was cheered by your simplest word?
Did you know that I longed for the smile on
    your face,
For the sound of your voice ringing true?
Did you know I grew stronger and better be-
    cause
I had merely touched shoulders with you?
I am glad that I live, that I battle and strive
For the place that I know I must fill;
I am thankful for sorrows, I'll meet with a
    grin
What fortunes may send, good or ill.
I may not have wealth, I may not be great,
But I know I shall always be true,
For I have in my life that courage you gave,
When once I touched shoulders with you.

*—Anon.*

———oOo———

# SELF-IMPROVEMENT

Welcome the task that makes you go beyond yourself.

*—Frank McGhie.*

———

The supreme h u m a n achievement is self-
mastery.

*—Anon.*

Accept criticism and seek counsel of those who will tell you your faults. Mere praise will never bring the improvement you need. He that won't be counseled can't be helped.

*—Anon.*

---

Kindness has more power than compulsion.

*—Anon.*

---

Benjamin Franklin conceived and proved the following plan for successful living which is taken from his famous autobiography:

"It was about this time I conceived the bold and arduous project of arriving at moral perfection. As I know, or thought I knew, what was right and wrong, I did not see why I might not always do the one and avoid the other. So I included under thirteen names, all that at that time occurred to me as necessary or desirable, and annexed to each a short precept.

1. Temperance—Eat not to dullness; drink not to elevation.

2. Silence—Speak not but what may benefit others or yourself.

3. Order—Let all your things have their places; each activity its time.

4. Resolution—Resolve to perform what you ought. Perform what you resolve.

5. Frugality—Make no expense but to do good to others and yourself.

6. Industry—Lose no time; be always employed in something useful.

7. Sincerity—Think and speak justly.

8. Justice—Wrong none by doing injuries, or omitting benefits that are your duty.

9. Moderation—Avoid extremes.

10. Cleanliness—Tolerate no uncleanliness in body, clothes, or habitation.

11. Tranquility—Be not disturbed at trifles, or at unavoidable accidents.

12. Chastity—Clean thoughts and wholesome activities lead to clean living.

13. Humility—Imitate Jesus and Socrates.

————

A Quaker friend kindly informed me that I was generally thought proud; that my pride showed itself frequently in conversation; that I was not content with being in the right when discussing any point, but was overbearing, and rather insolent, of which he convinced me by mentioning several instances; I determined to cure myself, if I could, of this vice or folly, and added Humility to my list, giving an extensive meaning to the word. I cannot boast of much success in acquiring the reality of this virtue, but I had a good deal with regard to the appearance of it. I made it a rule to forebear all direct contradiction to the sentiments of others, and all positive assertion of my own. I even forbade myself the use of every word or expression in the language that imported a fixed opinion, such as certainly, undoubtedly, and I adopted, instead of them, I conceive, I apprehend, or I imagine a thing to be so or so; or it so appears to me at present. When another asserted something t h a t I thought an error, I denied myself the pleasure of contradicting him abruptly, and in answering I began by observing that in certain cases his opinion would be right, but in the present case there appeared to me some difference. I soon found the advantage of this change in my manner; the conversations I engaged in went on more pleasantly. The way in which I proposed my opinions procured them a readier reception and less contradiction; I had l e s s mortification when found to be in the wrong, and I more easily prevailed with others to give up their mistakes and join with me when I happened to be in the right.

*—An excerpt from PGL ʾNo. 42.*

My intention being to acquire the habitude of all these virtues, I judged it would be well not to distract my attention by attempting the whole at once, but to fix it on one of them at

a time; and, when I should be master of that,
then to proceed to another, and so on, till I
should have gone through the thirteen; and as
the previous acquisition of some might facili-
tate the acquisition of certain others, I ar-
ranged them with that view, as they stand
above. Temperance first, as it tends to procure
that coolness and clearness of head, which is
so necessary where constant vigilance was to be
kept up, and guard maintained against the un-
remitting attraction of ancient habits, and the
force of perpetual temptations. This being ac-
quired and established, silence would be more
easy. This and the next, Order, I expected would
allow me more time for attending to my project and my studies. Resolution, once become
habitual, would keep me firm in my endeavors;
Frugality and Industry freeing me from my re-
maining debt, and producing affluence and in-
dependence, would make more easy the practice of Sincerity and Justice, etc. Conceiving
that daily examination would be necessary, I
contrived the following method for conducting
that examination.

I made a little book, in which I allotted a
page for each of the virtues. I ruled each page
with red ink, so as to have seven columns, one
for each day of the w e e k. I crossed these
columns with thirteen red lines, one for each
of the virtues, on which line, and in its proper
column I marked by a black spot 'every fault

I found upon examination to have been committed respecting that virtue upon that day.

I determined to give a week's strict attention to each of the virtues successively. Thus, in the first week, my great guard was to avoid even the least offense against Temperance, leaving t h e other virtues to their ordinary chance, only marking every evening the faults of the day. Thus, if in the first week I could keep my first line, marked Temperance, clear of spots, I supposed the habit of that virtue so much strengthened, and its opposite weakened, that I might venture extending my attention to include the next, Silence, and for the following week keep both lines clear of spots.

It was my design to explain and enforce this doctrine, that vicious actions are not hurtful because they are forbidden, but forbidden because they are hurtful, the nature of man alone considered; that it was, therefore, everyone's interest to be virtuous who wished to be happy in this world; and I should, from this circumstance, have endeavored to convince young persons that no qualities were so likely to make a poor man's fortune as those of probity and integrity.

————

Every life should have a blueprint—just as each bit of architecture must have. A life without a plan is like a ship without a compass. It gets nowhere because it lacks direction. Consider what you desire to be and to accomplish. Give sustained attention to the great decisions —religion, occupation, marriage, the choice of a home, avocation. Learn from your weaknesses and mistakes. Study the lives of others. Note what helped them most, what hindered them. Look at your life as a whole. Think of your expected seventy years in ten - year periods. Note what should be the character and achievement of the period between birth and ten years of age; between ten a n d twenty; between twenty and thirty; between thirty and forty; and so on. Include provision for each phase of your life. Revise your plan as conditions change. Careful and constant planning is the way to freedom.

*—Elmer Joy Morgan.*

Ah, but a man's reach should exceed his grasp, or what's a heaven for?

*—Robert Browning.*

Self - inspection is the best cure for self-esteem.

*—Wordsworth.*

## GETTING AROUSED

What I need most is someone to make me do what I can—not what Lincoln did but what I can do.

*—Emerson.*

Before water generates steam, it must register 212° of heat; 200° will not do it. The water must boil to generate enough steam to move an engine. Lukewarm water will not run anything. Lukewarmness will not generate life's work.

———

## THE WAGE

I bargained with life for a penny,
    And life would pay no more,
However, I begged at evening,
    When I counted my scanty store,
For life is a just employer,
    He gives you what you ask,
But once you have set the wages,
    Why, you must bear the task.
I worked for a menial's hire,
    Only to learn, dismayed,
That any wage I had asked of life,
    Life would have paid.

—*Jessie B. Rittenhouse.*

———

A certain young man had an unfortunate court experience which he felt would scar his soul for life. Although not entirely guilty he made preparation to leave the state. A friend, learning of his intentions dissuaded him from going by relating the following story:

Years ago, two brothers were guilty of sheep stealing. The ancient punishment was to brand the offender on the forehead, with the letter "S" to signify sheep stealer.

One brother left the state, but the other brother chose to remain in his home town and live down his mistake.

His repentance was so complete that, years later, a stranger inquiring about the meaning of the emblazed letter, was told unhesitatingly, "it stands for saint."

---

## GRUDGES

Just as it takes two to enter into a partnership, so it takes two to dissolve it; likewise, friendship cannot be broken without the aid and consent of both parties.

A schoolmate recently remarked, when I inquired concerning her friend of long standing, "I don't speak to her any more." I couldn't believe that anyone who had shared deep friendship, kindnesses, mutual profit, and happiness, as they had, could possibly dissolve such harmony and association. All the beauty of their friendship was destroyed because of one misunderstanding. Imagine letting one error stand against a thousand kindnesses and helpful actions of years of association!

A friendship which they had cultivated during their whole lifetime should not be dispensed within a moment.

I urged her not to destroy a thing so precious, for to hold a grudge is human; but "to forgive is divine" and is required of us from the Man of Nazareth.

———————

A man cannot speak, but he judges himself. With his will or against his will he draws his portrait to the eye of his companion by every word. Every opinion reacts on him who utters it. It is a thread-ball thrown at a mark, but the other end remains in the thrower's bag. Or, rather, it is a harpoon thrown at the whale, unwinding, as it flies, a coil of cord in the boat, and, if the harpoon is not good, or not well thrown, it will go nigh to c u t the steersman in twain or to sink the boat.

—*Emerson.*

———oOo———

# SELF-PITY

It appears more becoming for a man to be singing with the larks in the sky than croaking with the frogs in the swamps.

There's always lots of other folks you can be sorry fer 'stead of yerself.

You can not bring prosperity by talking poverty.

*—Quotations of Mildred Seydell.*

———oOo———

# SLANDER

No soul of high estate can take pleasure in slander. It betrays a weakness.—*Pascal.*

Little minds speak of persons; average minds of events; and great minds of ideas.—*Pascal.*

———

If you must slander, don't say it, but write it in the sand near the water's edge.

*—Napoleon Hill.*

———

Gossip has been well defined as putting two and two together and making five.

*—Pascal.*

———

I hold it to be a fact, that if all persons knew what each said of the other, there would not be four friends in the world.

*—Pascal.*

———

When a bee stings, she dies. She cannot sting and live. When men sting, their better selves die. Every sting kills a better instinct. Men must not turn bees and kill themselves in stinging others.

—*Bacon.*

These six things doth the Lord hate: yea, seven are an abomination unto him:

A proud look, a lying tongue, and hands that shed innocent blood,

An heart that deviseth wicked imagination, feet that be swift in running to mischief,

A false witness that speaketh lies, and he that soweth discord among brethren.

—*Prov. 6:16-20.*

Tale bearers are as bad as tale makers.

—*Sheridan.*

Where lies are easily admitted, the father of lies is not easily kept out.

—*Anon.*

No accurate thinker will judge another person by that which the other person's enemies say about him.

—*Napoleon Hill.*

Calumny would soon starve and die of itself if nobody took it in and gave it lodging.

—*Leighton.*

He who has injured thee was either stronger or weaker than thou. If weaker, spare him; if stronger, spare thyself.

*—Seneca.*

———

He that cannot forgive others breaks the bridge over which he himself must pass if he would ever reach heaven, for everyone has need to be forgiven.

*—Herbert.*

———

Never does a man portray his own character more vividly than in his manner of portraying another.

*—Richter.*

———

## HEARSAY

In every town, in every street,
In nearly every house you meet
A little imp, who wriggles in,
With half a sneer and half a grin,
And climbs upon your rocking chair
Or creeps upon you anywhere;
And when he gets you very near,
Just whispers something in your ear,
Some rumor of another's shame,
And little "Hearsay" is his name.

He never really claims to know;
He's only heard that it is so;

And then he whispers it to you,
So you will go and whisper too,
For if enough is passed along,
The rumor even though it's wrong,
If John tells Henry; Henry, Flo;
And Flo tells Mildred, and Mildred.
    Ruth;
It very soon may pass for truth.

You understand this little elf;
He doesn't say he knows himself;
He doesn't claim it's really true;
He only whispers it to you
Because he knows you'll go and tell
Some other whisperers as well;
And so before the setting sun
He gets the devil's mischief done,
And there is less of joy and good,
Around your little neighborhood.

Look out for "Hearsay" w h e n he
    sneaks
Inside the house when Slander speaks,
Just ask the proof in every case;
Just ask the name, the date, the place;
And if he says he only heard,
Declare you don't believe a word
And tell him that you'll not repeat
The silly chatter of the street.
However gossips smile and smirk,
Refuse to do the devil's work!

*—Author Unknown.*

# SORROW

Sorrow, like rain, makes roses and mud.
                    —*Austin O'Malley.*

---

Be still, sad heart! and cease repining;
Behind the clouds is the sun still shining;
Thy fate is the common fate of all;
Into each life some rain must fall;
    Some days must be dark and dreary.
                    —*Longfellow.*

---

Who never mourn'd hath never known
    What treasures grief reveals,
The sympathies that humanize,
    The tenderness that heals,

The power to look within the veil,
    And learn the heavenly lore,
The keyword to life's mysteries
    So dark to us before.
                    —*Author Unknown.*

---

When all our hopes are gone,
'Tis well our hands must still keep toiling on
    For others' sake;
For strength to bear is found in duty done,
    And he is blest indeed who learns to make
    The joy of others cure his own headache.
                    —*Author Unknown.*

# SUCCESS

You can't fell trees without some chips.
You can't achieve without some slips.
Unless you try, you'll wonder why
Good fortune seems to pass you by.
Success is not for those who quail
She gives her best to those who fail
And then with courage twice as great
Take issue once again with fate.
'Tis better far to risk a fall
Than not to make attempt at all.

—*Anon.*

He has achieved success who has lived well, laughed often, and loved much; who has gained the respect of intelligent men, and the love of little children; who has filled his niche and accomplished his task; who has left the world better than he found it, whether by an improved poppy, a perfect poem, or a rescued soul; who has never lacked appreciation of earth's beauty or failed to express it; who has always looked for the best in others and given the best he had; whose life was an inspiration; whose memory a benediction.

—*Bessie A. Stanley.*

Success and suffering are vitally and organically linked. If you succeed without suffering, it is because someone suffered for you; if you suffer without succeeding, it is in order that someone else may succeed after you.

—*Edward Judson.*

## ALPHABET OF SUCCESS

Attend carefully to details.
Be prompt in all things.
Consider well, then decide positively.
Dare to do right, fear to do wrong.
Endure trials bravely.
Go not into the society of the vicious.
Hold integrity sacred.
Injure not another's reputation.
Keep your mind free from evil thoughts.
Lie not for any consideration.
Make a few special acquaintances.
Never try to appear what you are not.
Observe good manners.
Pay your debts promptly.
Question not the veracity of a friend.
Respect the counsel of your parents.
Sacrifice money rather than principle.
Touch not, taste not intoxicating drinks.
Use leisure for improvement.
Venture not upon the threshold of wrong.
Watch carefully over your passions.
Extend to everyone a kindly greeting.

Yield not to discouragement.
Zealously labor for the right, and success
  is certain.

—Anon.

———

Whom, then, do I c a l l educated?
First, those who control circumstances
instead of being mastered by them,
Those who meet all occasions manfully,
and act in accordance with intelligent
thinking, those who are honorable in
all dealings, who treat good naturedly
persons and things that are disagreeable, and furthermore, those who hold
their pleasures under control and are
not overcome by misfortune, finally
Those who are not spoiled by success.

—Isocrates.

# TEACHING

The true aim of everyone who aspires to be
a teacher should be, not to impart his own
opinions, but to kindle minds.

Scratch the green rind of a sapling or wan-
tonly twist it in the soil, and a scarred or
crooked oak will tell of the act for centuries

to come. So it is with the teachings of youth, which make impressions on the mind and heart that are to last forever. The highest function of the teacher consists not so much in imparting knowledge as in stimulating the pupil in its love and pursuit. To know how to suggest is the art of teaching.

*—Amiel.*

Win hearts, and you have all men's hands and purse's.

*—Burleigh.*

The most wonderful work in all the world is not to take iron and steel and cogwheels and make a locomotive or a watch. Nor is it to take pen and parchment and write an Iliad. Nor is it to take paint and brush and canvas and paint an Angelus. But an infinitely greater task than all this is to take an ignoble, dishonest man and transform him into an upright lovable and honest man. Here we touch the creative power of the Galilean and bow before the mysteries of God.

*—George R. Wellington.*

## A TEACHER'S INFLUENCE

It was a good many years ago when a teacher came to a village school in the state of Indiana. That school was quite run-down. It had a reputation of getting rid of teachers. The school was gang-ridden by a dozen or more rough boys. The first day the teacher discovered the leader of the gang drawing rude pictures on a slate.

The teacher realized the crude caricature was of himself. The boy, bent over his slate, drawing between spasms of laughter, looking up at the teacher, then around the room, and back at the slate, was attracting the attention of the whole school.

When school was out for the day, this boy was requested to remain. He was the gang leader, and his partners in mischief gathered around the building, waiting to see what would happen between him and the new teacher. He had insulted the teacher the first day, and surely something drastic would be done. They were disappointed when after a few minutes he emerged from the building, smiling, and with a new book in his hand, made straight for home. This boy had never thought enough about books to carry one home. But something had really happened to that boy. He had met a truly great teacher.

That teacher had said to him: "James, I see that you have in you the making of a great artist or painter, maybe a poet. You have something every boy doesn't have. Here's a book. Take it home, read it, then draw for me the characters in the book as you see them."

That was all. The boy was waiting for the teacher the next morning. "Did you read any of the book?" asked the teacher.

"Any of it? I read all of it. Here's your drawing, too."

That teacher had done something to that boy—who was James Whitcomb Riley—and this experience was the turning point in his life. It was the influence of this one teacher that saved the Indiana genius who, all the neighbors said, "would come to some bad end."

The years went on, and Riley had become famous and greatly loved all over the land. He was living in Indianapolis, each day going to his office on an upper floor of a hotel in an elevator. The elevator boy said to him one day. "Mr. Riley, I understand you write poetry."

"Well, yes, I suppose; that is, I try."

"I, too, write poetry sometimes," answered the obscure boy. "Guess it's no good, but I likes to write it. My mother reads it, then I burn it."

"Bring your next poem to me," replied Riley, as he stepped out of the elevator. The boy was elated that the great Riley noticed him. Within a few days the boy was knocking at Riley's door. He showed Mr. Riley some poems he had written. Trembling and too frightened to say anything, he thrust them at the poet and tried to get out; but Mr. Riley closed the door and kept him in. He remained with that boy a whole hour. The boy was Paul Laurence Dunbar, and Riley's influence that day lifted that boy out of an elevator into the big world where he could be heard and in turn influence thousands of other lives.

A teacher of good influence becomes eternal in the lives of his students. Could anyone wish a greater reward?

—*W. G. Montgomery.*

## I TAUGHT THEM ALL

I have taught in high school for ten years. During that time I have given assignments, among others, to a murderer, an evangelist, a pugilist, a thief, and an imbecile.

The murderer was a quiet little boy who sat on the front seat and regarded me with pale blue eyes; the evangelist, easily the most popular boy in the school, had the lead in the junior play; the pugilist lounged by the window and let loose at intervals a raucous laugh that startled even the geraniums; the thief was a gay-hearted Lothario with a song on his lips; and the imbecile, a soft-eyed little animal seeking the shadows.

The murderer awaits death in the state penitentiary; the evangelist has lain a year now in the village churchyard; the pugilist lost an eye in a brawl in Hong Kong; the thief, by standing on tiptoe, can see the windows of my room from the county jail; and the once gentle-eyed little moron beats his head against a padded wall in the state asylum.

All of these pupils once sat in my room, sat, and looked at me gravely across worn brown desks.

I must have been a great help to those pupils—I taught them the rhyming scheme of the Elizabethan sonnet and how to diagram a complex sentence.

—*Naomi John White.*

---

## A PARABLE

I took a little child's hand in mine. He and I were to walk together for a while. I was to lead him to Father. It was a task that overcame me, so awful was the responsibility. And so I talked to the child lonely for the Father.

I painted the sternness of his face were the child to do something that would appease the Father's wrath. He walked under the tall trees. I said the Father had power to send them crashing down, struck by his thunderbolts. We walked in the sunshine; I told him of the greatness of the Father, who made the burning, blazing sun. And one twilight we met the Father. The child hid behind me. He was afraid. He would not look up at the face so loving, so remembered my picture. He would not take the Father's hand. I was between the child and the Father. I wondered I had been so conscientious, so serious.

———

I took a little child's hand in mine. I was to lead him in to the Father. I felt burdened with a multiplicity of the things I had to teach him. We did not ramble; we hastened from one spot to another spot. At one moment we compared the leaves of the different trees. In the next we were examining a bird nest. While the child was questioning me about it, I hurried him away to chase a butterfly. Did he chance to fall asleep, I awakened him, lest he should miss something I wished him to see. We spoke to the Father, oh, yes, often and rapidly. I poured into his fears all the stories he ought to know, but we were interrupted often by the wind blowing, which we must trace to its source. And then, in the twilight, we met the

Father. The child merely glanced at him and then his gaze wandered in a dozen directions. The Father stretched out his hand. The child was not interested enough to take it. Feverish spots burned in his cheeks. He dropped exhausted to the ground and fell asleep. Again I was between the child and the Father. I wondered. I had taught him so many things.

———

I took a little child's hand to lead him to the Father. My heart was full of gratitude for the glad privilege. We walked slowly. I suited my steps to the short steps of the child. We spoke of the things the child notices. Sometimes we picked the Father's flowers and stroked their soft petals and loved their bright colors. Sometimes it was one of the Father's birds. We watched it build its nest. We saw the eggs that were laid. We wondered, elated at the care it gave its young. Often we told stories of the Father. I told them to the child, and the child told them again to me. We told them, the child and I, over and over again. Sometimes we stopped to rest, leaning against one of the Father's trees, and letting his cool air cool our brows, and never speaking. And then, in the twilight, we met the Father. The child's eyes shone. He looked lovingly, trustingly, eagerly up to the Father's face. He put his hand into the Father's hand. I was for the moment forgotten. I was content.

—*Margaret L. White.*

## THE SPOILED BOY

He wheedled his mother and wheedled his dad
Who threatened but never did punish the lad.
They carried the burdens his shoulders should
    bear.
They solved all his problems and softened his
    care.
To keep the boy happy they faithfully tried.
But the more he was pampered the louder he
    cried.

When he fought with his playmates they ran
    to his aid.
They excused every failure in school that he
    made.
They blamed the poor teachers; they moved
    him about
From schoolroom to schoolroom, and never
    found out
That the reason he couldn't subtract or divide
Was always they ran to his help when he cried.

Now he blunders alone since they've both passed
    away,
For no one pays heed to his whining today.
He's a spiritless creature love labored to spoil,
Too timid to battle, too careless to toil.
For his parents forgot as they ran to his
    cry,
Just how helpless he'd be should they happen
    to die.

*—Edgar A. Guest.*

Ten Questions Parents Should Answer Correctly If They Want Their Children To Have Confidence In Them:

1. Are you babying the child rather than encouraging him to do things for himself?

2. Are you making his life tense rather than relaxed?

3. Are you giving out more disapproval than praise?

4. Are you pushing the child beyond his abilities rather than realizing his limitations?

5. Are you aloof rather than friendly with the child?

6. Are you riding the child on his weaknesses rather than trying to improve them?

7. Are you holding up a superior child as an example rather than comparing the child to someone nearer his own abilities?

8. Are you setting an "I can't" example rather than exhibiting self-sufficiency yourself?

9. Are you overly protecting the child rather than teaching him responsibility?

10. Are you letting the child withdraw from situations he should be made to face?

*—B. Von Haller Gilmer.*

# TIME

Dost thou love life? Then do not squander time, for that is the stuff life is made of.

—*Benjamin Franklin.*

And the plea that this or that man has no time for culture, will vanish as soon as we desire culture so much that we begin to examine seriously into our present use of time.

—*Matthew Arnold.*

Lost! Somewhere between sunrise and sunset, two golden hours, each set with sixty diamond minutes. No reward is offered, for they are gone forever.

—*Horace Mann.*

It is asked, how can the laboring man find time for self culture? I answer, that an earnest purpose finds time, or makes it. It seizes on spare moments, and turns fragments to golden account. A man who follows his calling with industry and spirit, and uses his earnings economically, will always have some portion of the day at command. And it is astonishing how fruitful of improvement a short season becomes, when eagerly seized and faithfully used. It has often been observed that those who have the most time at their disposal profit by it the least.

—*Channing.*

———

Lost wealth may be regained by industry, and economy, lost knowledge by study, lost health by temperance and medicine, but lost time is gone forever.

—*Horace Mann.*

———

## VALUE OF TIME

"What is the price of that book?" at length asked a man who had been dawdling for an hour in the front store of Benjamin Franklin's newspaper establishment. "One dollar," replied the clerk. "One dollar," echoed the lounger; "can't you take less than that?" "One dollar is the price," was the answer.

The would-be purchaser looked over the books on sale awhile longer, and then inquired; "Is Mr. Franklin in?" "Yes," said the clerk. "He is very busy in the press-room." "Well, I want to see him," persisted the man. The proprietor was called, and the stranger asked: "What is the lowest, Mr. Franklin, that you can take for that book?" "One dollar and a quarter," was the prompt rejoinder. "One dollar and a quarter! Why, your clerk asked me only a dollar, just now." "True," said Franklin, "and I could have better afforded to take a dollar than to leave my work."

The man seemed surprised; but, wishing to end a parley of his own seeking, he demanded: "Well, come now, tell me your lowest price for this book." "One dollar and a half," replied Franklin. "A dollar and a half! Why, you offered it yourself for a dollar and a quarter." "Yes," said Franklin coolly, "and I could better have taken that price then than a dollar and a half now."

The man silently laid t h e money on the counter, took his book, and left t h e store, having received a salutary lesson from a master in the art of transmuting time, at will, into either wealth or wisdom.

*—Orison Marden.*

———

We often say, "There are just a few minutes before mealtime; there is no time for anything now."

Out of the fragments of time that most of us waste—some have learned languages, have written books, have become learned.

Longfellow translated the *Inferno* by snatches of ten minutes a day, while waiting for his beverage to boil.

One hour daily would make an ignorant man well informed in ten years.

# TRANSGRESSION

Sin is never at a stay; if we do not retreat from it, we shall advance in it; and the farther on we go, the more we have to come back.

—*Barrow.*

---

As sins proceed they ever multiply; and like figures in arithmetic, the last stands for more than all the rest that went before.

—*T. Browne.*

---

There is no sin we can be tempted to commit, but we shall find a greater satisfaction in resisting than in committing.

—*Howell.*

---

Bad men hate sin through fear of punishment; good men hate sin through their love of virtue.

—*Juvenal.*

---

It is not only what we do, but also what we do not do, for which we will be held accountable.

—*Moliere.*

---

Sins are like circles in the water when a stone is thrown into it; one produces another.

When anger was in Cain's heart murder was not far away.

*—Philip Henery.*

If I grapple with sin in my own strength, the devil knows he may go to sleep.

*—H. J. Adams.*

It is not true that there are no enjoyments in the ways of sin; there are, many and various. But the great and radical defects of them all is, that they are transitory and unsubstantial, at war with reason and conscience, and always leave a sting behind. We are thirsty, and they offer us drink; but it is from deadly fountains. We are hungry, and they offer us bread; but it is poisoned bread. They may and often do satisfy us for a moment; but it is death in the end. It is only the bread of heaven and the water of life that can so satisfy that we shall hunger no more and thirst no more forever.

*—Tryon Edwards.*

God had one son on earth without sin, but never one without suffering.

*—Augustine.*

It is trial that proves one thing weak and another strong. A house built on the sand is in

fair weather just as good as if built on a rock.
A cobweb is as good as the mightiest cable
when there is no strain upon it.

*H. W. Beecher.*

———

Too much sun makes a desert.

—*An Arabian proverb.*

———

## SIN

Sin is essentially a departure from God.

—*Luther.*

———

He that falls into sin is a man, he that grieves
at it is a saint, he that boasteth of it is a
devil.

—*Fuller.*

———

Sin is first displeasing, then it grows easy,
then delightful, then frequent, then habitual,
then confirmed; then the man is impenitent,
then he is obstinate, then he is resolved never
to repent, and then he is ruined.

—*Leighton.*

———

If thou wouldst conquer thy weakness, thou
must never gratify it—no man is compelled to
evil; only his consent makes it his. It is no

sin to be tempted; it is to yield and be overcome.

—Penn.

———

He who sins against men may fear discovery, but he who sins against God is sure of it.

—Jones.

———

You can't go through the mill without getting dust on you.

—Jacob Probst.

———

The greatest sin of all is to be conscious of none.

—Carlyle.

———

## THE STAIN

You can't paint black and not get black,
   No matter how hard you try,
You may paint with care, but the stains are
     there,
   And stay when the paint is dry.

You can't fool around where the sinner's found,
   Make friends of the foolish kind,
But it leaves some taint, like the mark of
     paint,
   On your heart or your soul or your mind.

You may say you can, and you may think you
    can,
    That you'll keep your own hands clean,
But it leaves a mark that is deep and dark,
    A mark that you have not seen,

For sin is a thing that will always cling,
    Though you only meant to play;
It will leave some stain on the heart or brain
    That is hard to wash away.

You can't paint black and not get black,
    You can't fool around with sin,
It will leave its trace on the human face,
    Its mark on the soul within.

By the words you use and t h e friends you
    choose,
    You are made for the years to be;
You may think they'll not, but they'll leave a
    blot,
    For the rest of the world to see.

*Anon.*

## THE TWO GLASSES

There sat two glasses filled to the brim
On a rich man's table, rim to rim.
One was ruddy and red as blood,
And one was clear as the crystal flood.
Said the glass of wine to the paler brother,
"Let us tell the tales of the past to each
    other.

I can tell of banquet and revel and mirth,
How the proudest and grandest souls on
    earth
Fell under my touch as though struck by
    blight,
Where I was king, for I ruled in might.
From the heads of kings I have torn the
    crown;
From the height of fame I have hurled men
    down.
I have blasted many an honored name;
I have taken virtue and given shame;
I have tempted the youth with a sip, a
    taste,
That has made his future a barren waste.
Far greater than any king am I
Or than any army beneath the sky;
I have made the arm of the driver fail,
And sent the train from the iron rail;
I have made good ships go down to sea;
And the shrieks of the lost were sweet to
    me;
For they said; "Behold, how great you be!
Fame, strength, wealth, genius before you
fall,
And your might and power are over all.
"Ho! Ho! pale brother," laughed the wine,
"Can you boast of deeds as great as mine?"
Said the water glass, "I cannot boast
Of a king dethroned or a murdered host;
But I can tell of a heart once sad,

By my crystal drops made light and glad;
Of thirst I've quenched and brows I've
    laved;
Of hands I have cooled and souls I have
    saved.
I have leaped through the valley, dashed
    down the mountain,
I flowed in the river and played in the
    fountain,
Slept in the sunshine, and dropped from the
    sky,
And everywhere gladdened the landscape
    and eye.
I have eased the hot forehead of fever and
    pain;
I have made the parched meadows grow
    fertile with grain;
I can tell of the powerful wheel of the mill,
That ground out the flour, and turned at
    my will;
I can tell of manhood debased by you,
That I have lifted and crowned anew.
I cheer, I help, I strengthen and aid;
I gladden the heart of man and maid.
I set the chained wine-captive free,
And all are better for knowing me."
These are the tales they told each other,
The glass of wine and paler brother,
As they sat together filled to the brim,
On the rich man's table, rim to rim.
                    —*Ella Wheeler Wilcox.*

A little neglect may breed mischief:
for want of a nail the shoe was lost;
for want of a shoe the horse was lost:
and for want of a horse the rider was
lost; being overtaken and slain by the
enemy; all for the want of a little care
about a horse shoe nail.

—*Benjamin Franklin.*

——oOo——

# TRIALS

A high character might be produced, I suppose, by continued prosperity, but it has very
seldom been the case. Adversity, however it
may appear to be our foe, is our true friend,
and, after a little acquaintance with it, we
receive it as a precious thing—the prophecy
of a coming joy. It should be no ambition of
ours to traverse a path without a thorn or
stone.

—*Charles H. Spurgeon.*

———

Trials, temptations, disappointments — all
these are helps instead of hindrances, if one
uses them rightly. They not only test the fibre
of character but strengthen it. Every conquer-
ed temptation represents a new fund of moral
energy. Every trial endured and weathered in
the right spirit makes a soul nobler and stronger than it was before.

—*James Buckham.*

The more the marble wastes, the more the statue grows. In shaping a beautiful character, life must waste you. Your trials are the hammer, your tribulations the chisel to knock off pride, and if that be so, why not now, and where you stand.

—*Robert Louis Stevenson.*

---

The great heart will no more complain of the obstructions that make success hard, than the iron walls of the gun which hinders the shot from scattering.

—*Emerson.*

---

The best rosebush after all, is not that which has the fewest thorns, but that which bears the finest roses.

—*Henry Van Dyke.*

---

To bear pain without letting it spoil your happiness is true valor.

—*Anon.*

---

Fire is the test of gold; adversity, of strong men.

—*Seneca.*

If thou faint in the day of adversity, thy strength is small.

—*Anon.*

If there is no conflict, I cannot gain a victory; if there is no victory, I cannot gain a crown of reward.

—*Joseph Smith.*

There will be no crown bearers in heaven who are not cross bearers on earth.

—*Anon.*

If you would not have affliction visit you twice, listen at once to what it teaches.

—*Burgh.*

To whom do we go, in times of trouble, for advice and consolation? . . . Amid calamity's storm and stress, we apply to men and women who have "come up through great tribulation," who are able, out of the wealth of their experience, to minister for our uplift and welfare. To them we go for counsel, for comfort, for the help which they, under God, are, alone qualified to give. They are his instruments for that purpose.

—*O. F. Whitney.*

## EXPERIENCE

I learn as the years roll onward
  And leave the past behind.
That much I have counted sorrow
  But proves our God is kind,
That many a flower I longed for
  Had a hidden thorn of pain,
And many a rugged bypath
  Led to fields of ripened grain.

The clouds that cover the sunshine
  They cannot banish the sun,
And the earth shines out the brighter
  When the weary rain is done.
We must stand in the deepest shadow
  To see the clearest light;
And often from wrong's own darkness
  Comes the weary strength of right.

We must live through the weary winter
  If we would value the spring.
And the woods must be cold and silent,
  Before the robins sing.
The flowers must be buried in darkness
  Before they can bud and bloom,
And the sweetest and warmest sunshine
  Comes after the storm and gloom.

So the heart from the hardest trial
    gains
  The purest joy of all,

And from the lips that have tasted
   sadness
The sweetest songs will fall,
For as peace comes after suffering,
   And love is reward of pain.
So after earth comes heaven,
   And out of our loss the gain.
                —*Author Unknown.*

——oOo——

# UNDERSTANDING

## FATHER FORGETS

Listen, Son: I am saying this as you lie asleep, one little paw crumpled under your cheek and the blond curls stickily wet on your damp forehead. I have stolen into your room alone. Just a few minutes ago, as I sat reading my paper in the library, a stifling wave of remorse swept over me. Guiltily I came to your bedside.

These are the things I was thinking, Son: I had been cross to you. I scolded you as you were dressing for school because you gave your face merely a dab with a towel. I took you to task for not cleaning your shoes. I called out angrily when you threw some of your things on the floor.

At breakfast I found fault, too. You spilled things. You gulped down your food. You put your elbows on the table. You spread butter too thick on your bread. And as you started off to play and I made for my train, you turned and waved a hand and called, "Goodbye, Daddy!" and I frowned, and said in reply, "Hold your shoulders back!"

Then it began all over again in the late afternoon. As I came up the road, I spied you, down on your knees, playing marbles. There were holes in your stockings. I humiliated you before your boy friends by marching you ahead of me to the house. Stockings were expensive —and if you had to buy them you would be more careful! Imagine that, Son, from a Father!

Do you remember, later, when I was reading in the library, how you came in, timidly, with a sort of hurt look in your eyes? When I glanced up over my paper, impatient at the interruption, you hesitated at the door. "What is it you want?" I snapped.

You said nothing but ran a c r o s s in one tempestuous plunge and threw your arms around my neck and kissed me, and your small arms tightened with an affection that God had set blooming in your heart and which even neglect could not wither. And then you were gone, pattering up the stairs.

Well, Son, it was shortly afterward that my paper slipped from my hands, and a terrible sickening fear came over me. What has habit

been doing to me? The habit of finding fault,
of reprimanding—this was my reward to you
for being a boy. It was not that I did not love
you; it was that I expected too much of youth.
It was measuring you by the yardstick of my
own years.

And there was so much that was good and
fine and true in your character. The little heart
of you was as big as the dawn itself over the
wide hills. This was shown by y o u r spon-
taneous impulse to rush in and kiss me good
night. Nothing else matters tonight, Son. I
have come to your bedside in the darkness, and
I have knelt there, ashamed!

It is a feeble atonement; I know you would
not understand these things if I told them to
you during your waking hours. But tomorrow
I will be a real daddy! I will chum with you,
and suffer when you suffer, and laugh when
you laugh. I will bite my tongue when impatient words come. I will keep saying as if
it were a ritual: "He is nothing but a boy—a
little boy!"

I am afraid I have visualized you as a man.
Yet as I see you now, Son, crumpled and weary
in your cot, I see that you are still a baby.
Yesterday you were in your mother's arms,
your head on her shoulder. I have asked too
much, too much.

*W. Livingston Larned.*

'Tis better to understand, than to be understood.

—*Anon.*

——oOo——

# WORRY

It ain't no use putting up your umbrella till it rains.

—*Alice Hegan Rice.*

———

Worry is interest paid on trouble before it comes due.

—*Dean Inge.*

———

Sufficient to today are the duties of today. Don't waste life in doubts and fears; spend yourself on the work before you, well-assured that the right performance of t h i s hour's duties will be the best preparation for the hours or ages that follow it.

—*Emerson.*

———

A useful formula for reducing worry was prescribed by a former university professor. He advocated asking three questions when you begin to worry:

First, "Is this my problem?" If the answer is no, forget it; don't worry. If the response is "yes," ask the second question, "Is this my problem now?" If the answer is "no," forget it; if it is "yes," ask the third question, "What can I do about it?" If there is something that can be done, do it. If nothing can be done, forget it; don't worry. Professor Cannon cited the following example: A student approaching an examination should ask the three above questions. In answer to the first question the student could answer, yes, it is my problem. Can I do anything about it? Yes, study hard. After the examination the answer to the third question is: "it is not my problem any longer." Providence itself cannot change the score. It is the teacher's problem to correct the paper, and all your worrying won't change things one iota— *So Quit Worrying.*

---

## REPUTATION

Reputation is what men and women think of us; character is what God and angels know of us.

*—Paine.*

---

The way to gain a good reputation is to endeavor to be what you desire to appear.

*—Socrates.*

# WORTH-WHILE STORIES

## KEEPING HIS WORD

One day a Spaniard who was talking to a Moorish student became very angry because the student challenged his religion. Pulling out his sword, the Spaniard said, "My God would not have such as you to live. Die, you coward!" and he killed him, leaving the body by the roadside.

As he was hurrying away, a band of students came down the road, and seeing what had been done, they started after the murderer. He knew the road better than they, and so, taking a hidden turn, he dropped over a wall into the garden of a wealthy Moor. Seeing the man working among his beautiful flowers, he ran to him, fell on his knees before him, and cried, "In my haste I have killed a man who loved not God. Save me from the mob at the gates! I have done what seemed right. Save me, I beg of you."

"If thou hast done wrong, thou should surely to be punished," said the old man, "but it is better to avenge oneself slowly. I will share with thee this peach which I have picked from the tree. When we have eaten together, thou canst be assured of my protection. When night cometh, I will come unto thee."

So saying, he locked the man in the garden

house and went to sit on his porch. Hardly had he seated himself when he heard the sound of many people who were wailing; they came nearer to his home; they knocked at his own gate; and the servant admitted them.

"What hast thou here?" asked the Moor as they entered his gate.

"We have the body of thy son, thine only son," answered a student, "for he hath been killed by a Spaniard not far away from thine own roadway. Let us leave him here and go quickly, that we may join in the search for the man who hath so wronged thee."

Without a word he let them all depart; then he shut himself in his room and fell on his face. This son was his one great joy in life, for all honored and loved him. In his garden house sat the man who had killed him. He had only to say the word, and the men would take him away and kill him. Should he say the word? Ah, but to that man he had promised life and liberty. They had eaten together; to wreak vengeance upon him was unthinkable, for he was a Moor. All day long he paced back and forth in the room that overlooked the sea, now black with wind and rain. In his soul there was a great storm.

As the mourners listened, they said one to another, "Behold, how he loved him. He grieveth even as a mother."

When night fell, he called all his servants to his room, and saying that he wished to be alone in his grief, he sent them each unto his own home. When the last one had gone, he went to the garden house and slowly unlocked the door.

As the man came forth, the Moor stood before him and said in a voice that made the prisoner tremble, "Thou art called Christian, yet thou hast killed my only son in thine anger; his body lieth there in my house. Thou oughtest to be severely punished, but I have eaten with thee. I gave thee my word, and my word shall not be broken. I leave thee to thine own God, believing that thou must answer to him for the breaking of his own law. Come!"

With trembling footsteps the old man led the young man to the street where one of his fleetish horses was ready for him to mount.

"Go," said the father. "Go far, while the night may be a help unto thee. God is just, and God is good. I thank him that I have no load such as thine to carry. It were easier to carry sorrow than shame. My son's memory shall be to me as the sunlight and the moonlight, as the fragrance of the violet and the beauty of the rose, as the cooling breeze on a weary day. Thou hast taken his life, but thou couldst not take away what he has been to his father. That is mine. Go, and may thine anger never again cause thee to break the law of thy God. Go."

As the sound of the swiftly moving horse's hoofs died away, the old man went again to stand by the bier of his son, his only son. "Better that thou are here than there, my son," he said. "And thy father hath still kept the faith that he taught unto thee."

—*Margaret White Eggleston.*

## TWENTY-FOUR GOLDEN HOURS

Try living for twenty-four hours
as if Christ were beside you.

Charlotte had come to a hard time in her life. She was filled with discontent. Everything seemed wrong. Her ambitions were thwarted; her friends were commonplace; her home unattractive, her own personality unlovely, as she was well aware. The problem was too much for Charlotte. She seemed caught in a current of circumstances that was carrying her into an ugly and unsatisfying life, and she could not escape.

She went to the one person who seemed to be leading the kind of life that she passionately desired, Margaret Ames, lovely, popular, gifted, and successful, lived in a cottage studio set in a flower garden. There she painted those charming little water colors which were in such demand that they were always sold in advance. And Margaret was so kind, so willing to help, that you dared go to her with your problems. In the charming studio Charlotte poured out the story of her heartache over her frustrated, unhappy life. She told all the details, the poverty, the ugliness, the disappointment about school, the unsympathetic family, the careless friends, her own lack of charm and beauty. Margaret after a gentle word of sympathy said, "You can change all that if you really have the will to do it."

"How? How?" cried Charlotte. "I'll do anything, no matter how hard."

"Will you, indeed? It is not hard at all, it only takes time. You see, you must sow the seed for another kind of life, and wait with patience for it to grow. Here is a test to see whether you truly have the will: Live for twenty-four hours as if Christ were right beside you, seeing everything that you do. Then come to me again, and we'll talk it over. Will you do that?"

Charlotte was a church member, but she never spoke of Christ like that—almost as if he were a neighbor that one might speak to.

Somewhat constrained and doubtful, she answered, "Yes, Mrs. Ames."

"Then come again tomorrow, sometime in the evening, and we'll talk about the change."

It was late afternoon when Charlotte went home. She knew that she was expected to help get the supper onto the table. She went to the drawer and took out a wrinkled tablecloth. When she spread it on the table, she noticed several soiled spots. And here she had her first thought of change.

"If Christ were going to eat with us, I wouldn't put on a soiled cloth," she said to herself.

She got a fresh cloth. And with the same thought she brought in a small bowl of flowers from the yard. She put the butter on a fresh plate instead of on the soiled one. She cut the bread with care. She mashed the potatoes, and beat them light, instead of putting them on plain boiled. She made her gravy smooth and rich. "If I'd known Christ would be here, I'd have managed sometime today to make a nice dessert," she thought. She hoped that it wasn't sacrilegious to think of Christ in connection with desserts.

"Company tonight?" asked her father, peering through his glasses as he came to the table.

"Just you, Daddy," smiled Charlotte. If

Christ were present, of course you'd smile at your family and show them your very best manner.

Her mother, worn and hot, and still dressed in her kitchen clothes, sat down, saying, "I don't know what's got into her to fix up so for just us. I suppose she's expecting someone to drop in before we're done."

Charlotte bit back a hasty retort. She and Mother hadn't been getting on well lately. It seemed that Mother wouldn't try to keep up-to-date, and that she never understood how a girl felt about things. Charlotte kept still until she thought of the proper thing to say in the presence of the unseen Guest. "I don't know of anyone I'd rather fix things up for than our own folks," she said.

The family simply stared for a minute. That wasn't like Charlotte. Then Father said, "That's right, Daughter. It's too bad we all don't think of that oftener." But Dick snickered.

Charlotte's anger flared. There is nothing more maddening than to be laughed at when one is doing one's best. In another moment a sharp retort would have started a quarrel. But just in time Charlotte said to herself, "Christ is here," and she said nothing aloud.

There was a short, uncomfortable silence. Dick was ashamed but wouldn't say so. But soon they were all talking quietly again.

"It is better," thought Charlotte, "to keep still when anyone e l s e is exasperating. A quarrel makes Mother really ill, and it gives me a headache, besides making me look like a beast. Besides, I think Dick's ashamed. I can tell, because he's so gruff."

"It's your turn to wash the dishes," said Agnes, when the two girls began to do up the work.

"All right," said Charlotte. Usually there was a sharp argument over whose turn it was. Charlotte got the water ready and began. Agnes continued to carry dishes out in silence. After a while she burst out: "It really was my turn, Charlotte. I was a selfish pig to let you begin. I'll take my turn tomorrow night, and the next."

"It's all right, Agnes. I really don't mind washing at all."

To her astonishment Charlotte knew that this was true. When you didn't mind washing, it ceased to be the hard job that it had formerly been.

In the living room Charlotte slipped a magazine out from the bottom of the pile and began to read. She had brought the magazine home herself, and she kept it under cover. After a few minutes she put it down. It was not an immoral sheet; indeed, it was considered entirely respectable, but it was trashy, lurid, sentimental, a world removed from the wholesome type of love story. "I wouldn't be reading this if Christ were sitting where he could read with me," she thought. And she carried it out, and put it in the wastepaper bag.

"Charlotte, O Charlotte," cried gay voices at the door. "Come on along. We're having an impromptu party at Lucy's house."

A party; should she go? Oh, yes! Christ went to parties. He seemed to like going, and he helped other people to h a v e a good time. All through the gay evening Charlotte kept her thought, "Christ beside me." She didn't think of herself very much. She helped the girls get the hasty lunch. She talked to a quiet and shy young man and drew him into the games. She took her turn at stunts and stories without self-consciousness, and she felt a genuine thrill when someone said in the dark ahead of her on the way home, "That Charlotte Dale is a lot of fun, isn't she?" She knew that the crowd hadn't been thinking her much fun lately.

It was Wednesday, a half holiday, when Charlotte began her experiment. On Thursday morning she went to work again. Charlotte was a saleswoman in a dry goods store. She disliked her job very much. She had wished to go to college, only Father's salary couldn't be stretched that far. After college she had hoped to be an interior decorator. To help make beautiful homes, she thought, would be interesting work. But her ambitions were perishing while she worked in the commonplace store.

"Christ beside me," she thought as she walked into the store among the chattering girls. She said good morning smilingly to all she met.

"What's happened to 'Miss High-hat?' She actually said good morning to me. Someone must have left her a gold mine, she looks so pleasant."

That was one of the comments she overheard behind her. It was rather a shock, for she saw what her fellow workers had been thinking about her. Then she noticed that Thelma Pavic looked as if she had been crying. She remembered that she had heard that Thelma's mother was sick.

"How's your mother, Thelma?" she asked.

Thelma's tears brimmed over. "Oh, she's bad today. And no one to stay with her. If I could only be home."

"Don't cry, Thelma. I believe I could do your work and mine, too. It isn't a very busy time now. I'll ask Mr. Tanner if I can't do it, and let you go home."

In a few minutes she was back to tell Thelma to go. Then she did a thing that astonished her, a thing that seemed to say itself without her planning it. "And Thelma, we'll both pray for her. Remember, Christ is right at hand, and he cares about suffering people."

"Oh, Charlotte! Will you? I'll pray too, all day."

The fussy customer was almost purple in the face with anger because she had asked for a certain article that the "stupid clerks" had not been able to find for her.

"I suppose you'll say that you haven't anything like this," she said, flinging a small piece of wash goods down on the counter. "It's my opinion you are all too lazy to look for what a body wants."

Charlotte simply despised fussy, rude customers. This one's flushed, angry face and generally frowzy make-up bespoke a woman of a most disagreeable type. Charlotte's first impulse was to give her her iciest answer, and to make as little effort as possible. But by this time her talismanic word had become almost automatic. "Christ beside me. He'd be kind even to people like that." She smiled at the woman. "I'll look for it, madam. I'm almost sure we have a small piece left."

She brought the goods, still smiling. "I'm so glad I could find it for you," she said sincerely.

The virago was tamed. She was smiling in return. "Well, you are one clerk with a head," she said emphatically. "Why don't they get more like you?" She probably meant heart instead of head. But at least here was a clerk of whom she heartily approved.

When the customer was gone, Charlotte noticed that Miss Crowell, the department head, was watching her.

"You get along better even with the rude ones if you're pleasant to them," observed Charlotte.

"I'll say you do," said Miss Crowell. "But I wish more of the girls would learn that. The job's a lot easier, and it takes less out of you if you're good-natured. There's nothing wears you out like fighting with your job."

The rest of the day was like that. Charlotte did two girls' work and was not tired. She met every customer with an eager interest to serve acceptably. Closing time came before she knew it.

At eight o'clock she sat in Margaret Ames' studio again.

"I tried it, Mrs. Ames, just as well as I could, and—well, it made everything different. I think I can see what you mean. Of course, it didn't change the things that are bothering me. I'm still poor, and can't go to school, and I live in an ugly house, and I don't know the sort of people I'd like to——"

"Ah, my dear! But you only started the seed-sowing twenty-four hours ago. When you first put the seed in, the garden doesn't look different, does it? But it's on the way to becoming different. In three months it will be bright with bloom, not drab with dull, brown earth. That will be the way with you. You say these handicaps in your life haven't changed. But you've started to change them. Can you keep on as you've begun, and 'wait patiently' for the Lord, as the Psalmist tells us? You will cease to be poor, and without opportunity. Friends will be drawn to you. Doors will open before you. Your surroundings will blossom into beauty. You have the magic word. It is Christ. Fretting or even effort doesn't change things very much; but Christ does. Just remember to keep your daily walk very close to him."

"I'm going to do it," said Charlotte.

—*Janet Craig.*